CYBERSECURITY HYGIENE FOR THE HEALTHCARE INDUSTRY

The basics in Healthcare IT, Health Informatics and Cybersecurity for the Health Sector

VOLUME 2

JAMES SCOTT

Cybersecurity Hygiene for the Healthcare Industry: The basics in Healthcare IT, Health Informatics and Cybersecurity for the Health Sector Volume 2

ISBN: 978-1-5192121-3-9

CONTENTS

PREFACE

As hospitals and the health sector as a whole continue to take advantage of the conveniences provided by the latest IoT (Internet of Things) technologies, little attention is focused on the expansive and virtually completely unprotected attack surface evolving from use of these technologies. A cybersecurity-centric culture and an evolving enforcement of proper cybersecurity hygiene are mandatory to create even the most basic secure environment. Conversations and training centering on HIPAA, health IT and healthcare informatics must include cybersecurity, sadly it rarely does and the victims are typically the patients.

Strangely, cyber-attacks such as Anthem and others like it were not technically sophisticated rather the exact opposite. Spear phishing, spoofed URLs and watering hole attacks are the primary means of obtaining legitimate admin credentials, thus offering up one's entire network to hackers on a silver platter. Including the position of CISO is pointless unless the staff is properly trained to identify the ingredients of basic social engineering and a malicious attack.

This series is meant to introduce cybersecurity into the curriculum of those studying HIPAA, healthcare IT and health informatics as the topics go hand in hand, yet the health sector and academia as a whole have continued to ignore this reality therefore continue to be an easy target for hackers and bad actors. A cybersecurity-centric culture must be injected into every aspect of the health sector. Precise and determined effort must be introduced to initiate a mandatory cybersecurity hygiene standard throughout this crucial component of our Nation's critical infrastructure. This series has been authored to intentionally introduce cybersecurity and health IT simultaneously in hopes that the health sector will enforce the same concept to its academic partners.

BOTNETS: WHAT ARE THEY? AND HOW TO PROTECT YOUR COMPANY FROM THEM

WHAT ARE BOTNETS?

Bot, a short form for robot, is an automated program which allows external sources to control a computer remotely. The user is usually not aware of the infection. When several computers are affected in this manner, they network together to form a botnet, which is under the covert control of a command-and-control server. A botmaster is usually in control of such a server.

Without the users' knowledge, their computers are hooked up to botnet, and the botmaster can then employ them for a variety of wicked purposes. Most botmasters use the bots in the botnets to accomplish up to three main goals, not particularly in the given sequence:

- Generating and sending E-mail spam;
- Stealing identity information, user credentials, credit card details, usernames and passwords;

- Launching DDoS or distributed denial of service denying legitimate users from accessing the sites of the service provider.

Usually, botmasters earn huge amounts from spammers when they send spam email messages via their botnets. Within the botnet, each computer may be sending only 10 messages at a time, which might not cause any alarms to be triggered. However, 10 thousand zombie computers acting as a botnet can send a million messages.

Once inside the network of the organization, it is easy for the attacker to steal identity information, details of credit cards, credentials of the individual users and usernames and passwords to sensitive sites such as banking and investments. With certain types of malware, the botmaster is able to monitor keystrokes of the users in the botnet and harvest their personal information. Among other things, the botmaster can even hijack the internet browser the user is working with.

The attacker or the botmaster can cripple entire websites and disallow legitimate users from reaching their targeted sites. Botnets can be used to create overwhelming traffic to a specific website, which clogs all the routes. This action maintains a DDoS attack until the website owner agrees to some demands from the botmaster.

HOW TO KNOW IF BOTNETS HAVE ATTACKED YOU

There are a few obvious signs that your computer has been co-opted by a botnet:

- The computer occasionally fails to respond to commands, crashes often and/or runs unusually slow;

- The internet or network connection is unusually slow;

- Even when you are not using the internet, there is considerable network activity;

- The computer is unable to access websites;

- There is a dramatic increase in the amount of spam you receive or generate;

- Your firewall occasionally alerts you about unknown processes and/or programs as they try to access the Internet.

HOW TO INSULATE COMPUTERS AGAINST BOTNETS

If you suspect your computer is showing signs of being hijacked as a botnet, you must download and run a malicious software detection tool, and scan for botnet infection.

If there is positive confirmation that your computer is indeed affected, you have the choice of removing it by yourself or enlisting the help of a computer security expert. To do it yourself, you will need to:

- Procure and install antimalware and antivirus software, and/or update your existing software;

- Use special removal tools such as AntiBot or RUBotted;

- Quarantine and delete any malware detected by these tools;

- Repeatedly scan your computer until all traces of malware are removed and there is no further symptom of botnet activity exhibited by your computer.

Once you have cleaned out your system, make sure you have an updated operating system, up-to-date application programs and a strong firewall alerting you whenever any process or program tries to access the internet.

REFERENCES:

1. Wallace, J., TopTen Reviews, Botnet Zombie Apocalypse: How to Protect Your Computer. Available from: <http://mac-internet-security-software-review.toptenreviews.com/how-do-i-know-if-my-computer-is-a-botnet-zombie-.html>. [2013].

2. Kilpatrik, I., Federation Against Software Theft, BOT-NETS AND HOW TO DEAL WITH THEM. Available from: <http://www.fastiis.org/kaleidoscope/article/id/555/botnets-and-how-to-deal-with-them/>. [April 2010].

3. Microsoft, Safety & Security Center, How to better protect your PC from botnets and malware. Available from: <http://www.microsoft.com/security/pc-security/botnet.aspx>. [2013].

HOW VULNERABLE IS THE HEALTHCARE SECTOR TO HACKERS?

Lagging behind in addressing known problems, the healthcare industry remains one of the most vulnerable in the country

Although the search for efficiency and improved care has taken the healthcare industry to the Internet in recent years, its medical devices and vulnerable hospital computers have been exposed to a wide variety of hacking in the process. According to security researchers, there are intruders waiting to exploit known gaps for stealing records of patients to then use them in identity theft schemes. They can even launch disruptive attacks to shut down critical hospital systems.

After conducting a one-year investigation on cyber-security, The Washington Post found that healthcare remains one of the most vulnerable sectors in the country, partly because of the delay in addressing known problems. The industry has a huge number of gaping security holes. If the financial industry were to handle security the way healthcare industry is now, they would be stuffing cash in mattresses under their beds.

In comparison with the military, corporate and financial networks, hospitals and other medical facilities have faced relatively few hacks - that is, up until now. In the recent months, terrorists, criminals, cyber-warriors and activist hackers are finding healthcare an increasingly inviting target. Officials with the Department of Homeland Security confirm this. According to these sources, there is a growing tendency towards loss or theft of medical information and patient safety, because of these vulnerabilities.

When researched more deeply, according to The Washington Post, security experts find the same trivial-seeming flaws affecting the healthcare sector today as those that hackers exploited earlier to penetrate the computers at Google, the Pentagon and financial network services. The study also revealed that two major causes of persisting vulnerabilities within the healthcare industry are the routine failure to fix these known software flaws for ageing technology, and a culture of healthcare workers, nurses and physicians that do not follow basic measures of security such as not using passwords, in favor of convenience.

EXAMPLES OF TRIVIAL VULNERABILITIES

There were some disturbing findings revealed in The Washington Post investigation. A hospital in Oklahoma has a system that operates an electronic medicine cabinet. Weaknesses in the software interface allowed any unauthorized user to take over easily.

Peace Corps worldwide is about to adopt OpenEMR, a management system for electronic medical records. The software has several security flaws to allow hackers to break in easily.

A medical center at the University of Chicago has an unsecure Dropbox site so that new residents can use their iPads to manage patient care. They use a single user name and password, both of which they published in an online manual.

NOT KEEPING PACE WITH CHANGING TECHNOLOGY

Industry practices have not kept pace with the fast changing technology. Government oversight is partly to blame for this. Although the Food and Drug Administration is responsible for overseeing medical devices, their most recent guideline on cybersecurity was published back in 2005.

The agency does tell hospitals to seek help from vendors for guidance on security of sophisticated devices. Although the agency encourages such updates, vendors are often unable to update FDA-approved systems. That leaves those systems vulnerable to potential attacks and people are very confused about the position of FDA.

The Washington Post investigation also noted that although a report by the Government Accountability Office reported vulnerability of insulin pumps and defibrillators to hacks, a year later, one researcher-hacker used a specialized search engine and discovered a wireless glucose monitor in Wisconsin that was linked to the Internet and open to hacking.

The healthcare industry is moving toward electronic health records systems, overseen by the Department of Health and Human Services. However, there are documented security vulnerabilities in the system.

Although the HHS health information technology standards committee is of the view that the healthcare industry is working hard to overcome their shortcomings, other researchers are skeptical. They claim that several security flaws identified in electronic health record systems two years ago are yet to be rectified. That leaves the system open to exploitation by skilled hackers.

THE ONGOING CONCERN

For over a decade now, cybersecurity of medical systems has been under the lens. However, as hospitals are increasingly adopting the use of wireless systems and electronic records to manage patient data, the issue has magnified.

According to The Washington Post, the ICSA Labs that tests for security products such as electronic health records for government certification, they do acknowledge healthcare systems rank near the bottom of the list. There are not many attacks, since typically attackers have been concentrating on money thus far. However, this finding should not make the industry complacent since identity theft is on the rise and patient information is sensitive to hacking. A faulty assumption among healthcare officials is that their networks offer too few financial enticements, or are too obscure to be of any interest to hackers.

THE ANECDOTES ARE MOUNTING

No one is exactly aware of how many intrusions occur at any given period. However, mounting anecdotes are causing concern. For example, during 2009 and 2011, malicious viruses infected medical devices at VA facilities at least 181 times. This was reported by DHS intelligence.

The Utah Health Department had their network server compromised, when a hacker gained access to Medicaid data belonging to 780,000 people and stole several of them. Computers in Eastern Europe were responsible and Utah officials say they have taken extensive measures to protect their patients.

THE STEP FORWARD

HHS has established an array of standards and to meet them, the law requires that independent labs certify electronic health records. However, the standards include only a few security provisions. The existing pattern of industry practices leaves commercial EHR systems vulnerable to exploitation, with only low skill levels sufficient to exploit. Experts urge rigorous security testing before certifying vendors of electronic health records for stimulus funding. That makes it clear that federal certification standards are not sufficient.

BRINGING UNIFORMITY TO THE WEB, MOBILE AND...

BRINGING UNIFORMITY TO THE WEB, MOBILE AND TELEPHONE CHANNELS FOR HEALTHCARE

Health service delivery all over the world is poised for a sea change. This is being triggered by the prolific use of mobile devices and wireless technologies in achieving the objectives of mHealth. On one hand, there is an exponential rise in the use of mobile technologies and applications. On the other, there are new opportunities coming up for integrating mobile health into currently existing eHealth services. Moreover, all this is being supported by the steady growth in the coverage of mobile cellular networks.

The International Telecommunication Union estimates that the low and middle-income countries of the world have over 70% of the five billion wireless subscribers overall. The GSM Association confirms that over 85% of the world's population can access commercial wireless signals, a feat even the electrical grid has found difficult to achieve.

Patients in under-served areas of both developing as well as developed countries can overcome human resource shortages in the health sector. They can use the video, imaging, data, text or voice functions of a mobile device to communicate or consult a health professional. This is applicable in other situations also such as for management of chronic diseases of patients unable to leave home.

SOCIAL MEDIA IS BRINGING IN NEW COMMUNICATIONS LANDSCAPES IN HEALTHCARE

In most of the world, people's perception of the healthcare industry is marred with mistrust and doubt. Several factors have led to this chronic viewpoint – lack of transparency, avoidable harm to patients, endless red tape, unnecessary care, widespread inefficiencies, wasteful spending and ceaseless intrusions from drug cartels.

For the first time, this new communication tool is helping patients engage positively and proactively with healthcare organizations. By identifying negativity, social media is helping to address the concerns and complaints, while harvesting positive sentiment.

All over the world, more and more people are increasingly turning to digital tools for maintaining their overall health. According to a recent Pew Research Center study, nearly 33% of American adults turn to the web for figuring out a medical issue, and an overwhelmingly large number of patients prefer digital health communications. However, of all the hospitals in the US, hardly 26% were active on social media.

According to a recent Price Waterhouse Cooper's report, patients are more trustful of social media communications from doctors rather than from drug companies, health insurers or hospitals. That indicates clinicians are still the central reference for patients, while remaining at the focus of communication models. However, considering the number of practicing physicians, very few of them are active on social media. Moreover, providers and physicians prefer to talk more among themselves via social media, rather than directly to the patients.

One of the spectacular ways social media is shaping communications can be seen in the formation of patient groups. Moreover, such patient groups are demanding a more meaningful role and greater transparency in patient/provider relationships. The relationship between providers and patients is also undergoing a sea change with people able to access more information on the web very easily. People are beginning to realize that several providers are inadequately prepared to deal with their request for information due to malpractice claims and HIPAA laws.

HOW ARE HOSPITALS USING DIFFERENT CHANNELS FOR IMPROVING COMMUNICATIONS?

Hospitals are finding that locating clinicians and knowing how and when they can communicate cuts down time loss dramatically. Unified communications with integrated collaboration and information technologies offers a key area for improvement in opportunities. Time-sensitive interactions through better communication technologies can help both the originator and the recipient of the communication.

Although the vast range of communication and information technologies available may contribute to communication complexity, hospitals are finding that they need health system wide technology portfolios while integrating with the improvements in technology.

No magic pill exists for providing a cure for a hospital struggling with communication challenges. However, with the right mix of technologies and changes in process, caregivers can communicate more efficiently and effectively. This will allow them to focus more on providing outstanding patient care.

UNDERSTANDING COMMUNICATION SYSTEMS WITHIN HEALTHCARE

Normally, communication systems within healthcare include people, messages, organizational structures and mediating technologies. Moreover, these systems may use formal or informal structures when supporting communication needs.

To start with, the channel forms the pipe along which messages are exchanged. These channels may be of a wide variety, ranging from the basic face-to-face conversations to telecommunication channels such as telephonic conversations or e-mail exchanges and computational channels such as the medical records. Channels are associated with attributes such as capacity and noise and these determine their suitability for different tasks. In addition, channels can be synchronous or asynchronous.

Telephones are an example of the commonest form of two-way synchronous communication channels – two parties can exchange messages across the channel at the same time. However, synchronous channels can be interruptive, with the interruptions having the capacity of creating a negative impact on individuals with high cognitive loads. For example, a clinician may have forgotten to carry out a clinical task because a telephone call had interrupted him when he was busy.

Individuals separated in time typically use asynchronous channels to communicate. Due to lack of simultaneous communication, they resort to a form of conversation based on a series of message exchanges. Some examples of this type of communications are Post-It notes left on the desk of a colleague and electronic messaging systems. The major advantage of asynchronous communication is that it is inherently non-interruptive, with the busy individual having a choice of ignoring non-urgent communication until a more convenient time.

In healthcare, the sender structures messages with an aim of achieving a specific task while using available resources to suit the needs of the receiver. There can be informal messages with variable structures that use voice and electronic messages, whereas formal or structured communication use formats such as hospital discharge summaries. Some of these messages may also be computer generated and typically following standard formats such as HL7, which is now the international messaging standard followed within healthcare.

Communication within healthcare can also be defined by formal procedures or policies as opposed to being governed by technology. There can be different policies within a hospital to define communication system performance, without being tied to any specific technology. For example, the policy may not allow a general practitioner to access medical records directly from the records department without the permission of the clinician.

Different information transactions may involve agents that build up the communication system. For example, a ward clerk fielding all telephone calls in a busy clinical unit. Here, the hospital's policy has created an organizational structure in the form of the clerk's specific communication role, which allows minimum interruption to the clinical staff. However, agents are required to have attributes such as understanding of language and specific tasks.

In communication systems within a hospital, the same channel can be used to handle different kinds of communication services. For example, the telephone line, although used primarily for voice communication, also serves for fax transmission and reception. Another example is a mobile phone being used for text messaging, image transmission in addition to providing voice-mail.

Hospital staff may use different communication devices to run communication systems. For example, a doctor may need to use a personal digital assistant, a fax machine and a telephone. Mostly, different tasks and situations call for the use of different devices. Sometimes, communication devices are small enough to be worn as personal accessories, such as patients wearing heart rate monitors and blood-pressure monitors.

Interaction mode is an important way in which interactions within a healthcare unit can be designed. For example, some communications may be very urgent and demand immediate attention – through the ringing tone of a mobile phone, while others are designed not to interrupt – a text message. However, the receiver may choose to convert the asynchronous service designed not to interrupt, to an interruptive interaction mode, such as by turning on the notifications on his or her mobile to generate a tone when a text message arrives. Of course, this alters the impact of the service on the message receiver.

In any healthcare unit, patient privacy concerns mandate that security protocols be followed so that unauthorized personnel cannot access clinical records. Communication systems may protect privacy by encoding messages to prevent them from being intercepted and interpreted by unscrupulous individuals. Similarly, medical reports sent over emails may be encrypted, so that only the recipient, who possesses a special key, can open, decode and read them. Usually, the choice of security protocol used depends on the degree of risk attached to unauthorized access of the message content.

CONCLUSION

The communication system used in a healthcare unit is largely dependent on the hospital - whether it is adequately prepared to take on positive and negative patient communication, on social media and on other channels. While larger hospitals can involve staff and resources to monitor and respond to positive and negative comments regularly, smaller healthcare units may not have adequate resources to respond timely. Hospitals with tighter budgets may have to revert to using free tools for monitoring social media to record patient sentiment.

REFERENCES

1. mHealth New horizons for health through mobile technologies http://www.who.int/goe/publications/goe_mhealth_web.pdf

2. Social Media And Healthcare: Navigating The New Communications Landscape http://binaryfountain.com/social-media-and-healthcare-navigating-the-new-communications-landscape/

3. Communication Systems in Healthcare http://www.ncbi.nlm.nih.gov/pmc/articles/PMC1579411/

YOUR BUSINESS CRITICAL APPLICATIONS ARE VULNERABLE TO SSRF ATTACKS

WHAT ARE BUSINESS CRITICAL SYSTEMS AND WHAT IS AN SSRF ATTACK?

Modern businesses run on business application infrastructure, with typical modules such as Enterprise Resource Planning or ERP, Customer Relationship Management or CRM and Supplier Relationship Management or SRM. These systems hold data related to personnel, financial and other sensitive information critical to the operation of the enterprise. Moreover, these systems are often connected to the Supervisory Control and Data Acquisition systems (SCADA) and/or banking client workstations.

Server Side Request Forgery or SSRF is an attack on existing vulnerability of the business application infrastructure. Attackers use a victim server interface that can send a packet to another host on another port and can be accessed remotely without authentication.

WHAT HAPPENS DURING AN SSRF ATTACK?

Business-critical systems are usually located in a secure subnetwork secured by firewalls and monitored by Intrusion Detection Systems, regularly patched for their vulnerabilities.

The ERP and other networks are usually separated from the corporate networks by a firewall. In turn, the corporate networks are protected from the Internet and cloud systems by another firewall. However, insecure systems have vulnerabilities existing between the corporate network and the ERP network, which attackers exploit.

During an SSRF attack, a compromised server sends a packet to a service, which then encloses another packet within the original packet and forwards it to another service. It is much like sending a forged letter hidden inside another letter. Much depends on how much the attacker can manipulate the contents of the second packet and that constitutes different types of SSRF attacks. There are typically two types of SSRF attacks: Trusted and Remote.

The trusted SSRF attacks can usually send forged packets or forged requests to predefined services. Remote SSRF attacks involve forged requests to any remote port or IP.

Trusted SSRF attacks are very stealthy, as most of the systems across the enterprise are linked through the secure sub network, and the behavior of the requests looks very normal. However, these attacks are somewhat difficult to make because they need an existing link and credentials such as usernames and passwords.

On the other hand, remote SSRF attacks are possible from a trusted source to any host and any port, even if the source cannot connect to the remote hosts directly. Attackers scan the remote hosts for open ports and IP addresses. If authentication is not required, it is possible to scan an internal network from the Internet. Remote SSRF threats can:

- Exploit Operating System and Data Base vulnerabilities
- Exploit the vulnerabilities of old ERP applications
- Bypass the security restrictions of ERP
- Exploit existing vulnerabilities in ERP local services

WHY IS AN SSRF ATTACK CRITICAL TO THE ENTERPRISE?

The company's critical information is stored in its ERP and this makes the attack on the ERP system very lucrative to a competitor, an industrial spy or a cybercriminal. The critical information may include intellectual property, information on public or customer relations, personally identifiable information and most importantly, financial data.

A business can suffer a significant amount of damage if the ERP system is compromised due to insider embezzlement, fraud, sabotage or industrial espionage.

HOW TO PREVENT SSRF ATTACKS

Most business critical systems require close collaborations with the vendor to close the vulnerabilities allowing SSRF attacks. Regular patching and use of continuous monitoring systems along with vulnerability assessment systems will help. It is preferable to use systems that can expose zero-day vulnerabilities.

Let application security experts assess the business critical systems and monitor the systems with automated solutions such as ERP-Scan Security Scanner. The scanner can identify misconfigurations, vulnerabilities, and many other issues.

REFERENCES:

1. Polyakov, A., *SSRF vs. Business critical applications.* Available from: <http://media.blackhat.com/bh-us-12/Briefings/Polyakov/BH_US_12_Polyakov_SSRF_Business_WP.pdf>. [?].

2. Polyakov, A., *SSRF: The new threat for business – critical applications.* Available from: <http://erpscan.com/wp-content/uploads/2012/09/SSRF-The-new-threat-for-business-critical-applications-from-RSA.pdf>. [2012].

3. Polyakov, A., *SSRF attacks in the limelight at ERPScan's press conference in China.* Available from: <http://erpscan.com/press-center/news/ssrf-attacks-in-the-limelight-at-erpscans-press-conference-in-china/>. [17 September 2012].

CYBERDRILL, THREATS AND HEALTHCARE CYBERSECURITY

Apart from the need to improve willingness to share cyber-security information, many healthcare organizations must also be willing to improve their basic cyber-security defenses.

A cyber-security drill conducted by the HHS or the Health and Human Services together with HITRUST or the Health Information Trust Alliance on April 1, 2014 resulted in findings that healthcare organizations should target improving their basic mechanism of defense against cyber-attacks. Simultaneously, they should also improve their willingness to share information regarding cyber threats. They have also studied the emerging threats facing the healthcare industry and the ongoing efforts towards its security by the HealthCare.gov.

CHALLENGES FACING THE HEALTHCARE SECTOR

The drill found that the healthcare ecosystem is no different from other sectors as far as the challenges it faces compared to what others do; the threats are common – hacktivism, state-sponsored threats, bad behavior from employees and organized crime – both intentional and unintentional. However, the difference where the healthcare sector stands out is that there exists a huge resistance towards implementation of best practices of information security, this being an additional challenge for the industry sector. Most often, on one hand, organizations are not willing to share information regarding their security breaches and incidents of cyber-crime. On the other, clinicians shun technologies such as multi-factor authentication.

A PEEK INTO THE CYBERRX DRILL

Information security teams conducted the recent CyberRX drill at several hospitals and health insurance companies, healthcare providers, a large nationwide retail pharmacy chain and 13 unnamed healthcare sector companies. Of the four exercises conducted, two involved a compromised medical device and ran for over a seven-hour period. They also included a simulated attack on a state health insurance exchange that was connected to the federally facilitated insurance marketplace belonging to the HealthCare.gov of the HHS.

Compared with others, the healthcare sector has an added risk. This sector is a complex web of hundreds of thousands of providers and a massive conglomerate of interconnected systems, devices, the government and acts such as the Affordable Care Act. According to the first set of exercises, the primary challenge in the healthcare sector is the concern of liability leading to reluctance in sharing information about attacks and threats with the rest of the sector.

As such the concern of liability is from a company standpoint, rather than from the cyber-security side. It boils down to the liability introduced into the company environment when information about a breach or other problems is shared. Healthcare organizations are concerned about what they share and how so that it does not cause them any liability.

This concern about liability is at the root of why there is not much sharing between industries, despite the executive orders from President Obama. The order encourages sharing between the private sectors, public sectors, and the federal government in order to improve cyber-security and situational awareness, while improving overall security.

Along with the reluctance to share information about cyber-threats, attacks and incidents, the first drill also indicated that many healthcare entities must still iron out their defense mechanisms. Basically, some participating organizations find that they have yet to set up proper processes and methods when dealing with an incident. This involves fundamentals such as basically knowing whom to call when an incident does occur.

Among the pool of participants, some organizations had mature programs, which they exercised, but several others did not, and realized the gaps. The next exercise to be conducted later in the year will have a larger sample size, which will enable examination of why some organizations are better prepared than others.

The drills have evoked a good response from more than 300 healthcare related organizations. This is especially so because the participants undergoing that drill found an opportunity to exercise their internal processes for incident response and ways to improve.

RESISTANCE TO BEST PRACTICES

Another finding of the drill is that the healthcare sector resists implementation of best practices as a whole, for information security. For example, physicians demonstrate a lot of resistance to the use of two-factor authentication.

Conducting drills such as CyberRX, together with education and communication, helps to make people understand the actual and real risks involved with such threats. Although there has been a lot of fear mongering, to date, HealthCare.gov has not faced any successful malicious attacks on their systems or on their site. Additionally, HealthCare.gov is currently undergoing comprehensive security testing every three months, even though the federal government has a guideline such rigorous testing take place every three years.

HealthCare.gov is likely to continue being tested every quarter for another year or two, before a reasonable cycle is decided. As insurers offer new health plans, the security team and HealthCare.gov will be busy updating the site and systems, with the process being a continual improvement for the site.

The healthcare sector is no different from other industries when it comes to emerging cyber-threats. Those include organized crime circles and threats posed by insiders involving theft of data to commit fraud. However, the healthcare sector faces additional threats from nation-states as well, where the focus of that threat is on stealing intellectual property.

The US healthcare sector has the best technologies, devices, software, drugs and electronic medical records under development. Nation states are mostly interested in IP, because they would not need to conduct their own research if they can steal from someone else.

ICD -10 AND MEANINGFUL USE OF ELECTRONIC HEALTH...

ICD -10 AND MEANINGFUL USE OF ELECTRONIC HEALTH RECORDS

Inconsistent quality and rising costs are only a few of the challenges that the US healthcare system faces regularly. Potentially, use of electronic health records will improve the effectiveness and efficiency of healthcare providers. While ARRA or the American Recovery and Reinvestment Act of 2009 prioritized a national, inter-operable health information system, the bipartisan support from US policymakers sped up its adoption.

The latest figures are detailed in the journal Health Affairs, published by the HHS office of the National Coordinator for Health Information Technology. According to this publication, in 2013, almost 78 percent of office-based physicians had adopted the EHR system in some form, while 59 percent of the US hospitals had adopted it.

ARRA includes several measures for modernizing the infrastructure of the nation, one of them being HITECH or the Health

Information Technology for Economic and Clinical Health Act. In turn, the HITECH Act supports the concept of electronic health records and their meaningful use, commonly known as EHR-MU. This is an effort led by ONC or Office of the National Coordinator for Health IT and CMS or Centers for Medicare & Medicaid Services.

According to the HITECH Act, the healthcare delivery system throughout the US should make meaningful use of inter-operable electronic health records, treating it as a critical national goal. It defines meaningful use as using certified EHR technology in a meaningful manner ensuring that there is provision for electronic exchange of health information to improve the quality of care and that the provider submits information on quality of care and other measures to the Secretary of Health & Human Services.

To expand on the concept still further, meaningful use has five priorities based on the health outcome policy:

- Improving the efficiency, safety and quality of health care while reducing divergence

- Interesting patients and families in their health and well-being

- Improving public and population health

- Developing care coordination

- Ensuring adequate security and privacy protection for personal health information

ELECTRONIC HEALTH RECORDS AND INTEROPERABILITY

Hospitals generate health information in one or several encounters with the patient in care delivery settings. They maintain this patient information as EHRs or Electronic Health Records. This data includes patient demographics, problems, vital signs, medication, past medical history, immunizations, progress notes, radiology reports and laboratory data. Clinicians use EHRs to automate and streamline their work flow as EHRs can generate a total history of the clinical encounter faced by the patient, while supporting other activities related to care directly or indirectly. Such activities include outcome reporting, quality management and evidence-based decision support.

HITECH stimulus provisions such as ICD-10 stressing on the meaningful use of EHRs are leading many physicians and hospitals towards adopting EHR systems for modernizing their operations. Along with the increase in EHRs, there is also a need for a sufficiently detailed and expandable standard code set to capture the data from current as well as future healthcare accurately. Therefore, ICD-10 cannot be considered a competing initiative, but an enabler to allow the healthcare industry to adopt EHR for building a data infrastructure. The nationwide healthcare system urgently needs this data infrastructure where pharmacies, laboratories, hospitals and clinicians can share PHI or patient health information electronically and securely.

According to CMS, interoperability can only be achieved effectively with standardized data. This will allow sharing information between different EHR and health plan systems. ICD-10 is one of many classification systems and referencing technologies that provide a uniform way of collecting and maintaining patient data.

In this evolving healthcare market, the emerging health economy is shifting from FFS or Fee-for-Service to P4P or Pay-for-Performance and P4V or Pay-for-Value models. Additionally, business systems impacted by this shift need upgrading and adjusting of associated costs so that they comply with multiple federal initiatives. In this context, the eHealth initiatives put forward by CMS are helping to meet the Triple AIM goals of improvement – leading to an increase in the efficiency of health delivery in the US.

CMS eHealth initiatives aim at improving healthcare delivery using simplified, standardized electronic information and technology. Along with other initiatives for simplification of administration,

ICD-10 will improve the quality and efficiency of electronic information exchanged between providers, Medicare and other players.

ICD-10 is instrumental in accelerating research, health status monitoring and in streamlining quality and interoperability. This in turn helps in unifying architectures for public health surveillance leading to an improvement in population health. Interoperability and effective sharing of clinical data requires a common medical language and this is provided by the amalgamation of terminologies and classification systems. Improved patient care coordination across the nation requires secure exchange of information between patients and providers. Initiatives such as eHealth will help advance such requirements.

EHRS, ICD-10 AND MANAGEMENT OF REVENUE CYCLE RISK

Following the newest ICD-10 release announcement, CMS has published ICD-10 testing opportunities for providers still operating with FFS. This is a comprehensive four-pronged approach that tests the Medicare FFS provider for ICD-10 and its preparedness. In this approach, the tests include:

- CMS Internal testing of the provider's claims processing systems
- Downloading CMS Beta testing tools
- Testing the provider's acknowledgements
- Testing the provider end-to-end

Before participating in CMS testing, organizations must first complete their internal testing to ensure that their own systems are operating correctly. This should include Revenue Cycle User Acceptance Testing, as this increases the likelihood of a successful test with CMS. Some lessons learnt from hospitals and health centers across the country employing a variety of strategies to protect revenues during transition to ICS-10 are as follows -

- Ensure representation of all key areas during the planning phase – include payers, charging, billing, IT and coding

- Ensure confirmation of payer requirements before test files are built

- Ensure available resources and time requirements are identified

- Ensure evaluation of test environments to make them available when scheduled for remediation

- Ensure evaluation of a test file for use with different payers

- Ensure validation of a test procedure by starting with a small test file

- Consider if test files will be copied from live billing systems or built manually – reporting trends may be tracked

- Evaluate 835s received from payers for monitoring testing results.

Healthcare organizations striving to manage the impact on resources must include in their initial tests only a limited number of claims with payers as test transactions. This will allow for a shorter learning cycle. For additional testing, it is necessary to include a good cross-section of everyday business as well as coding scenarios related to specialties with expanded code sets. It would be prudent to set the testing team's goal to complete end-to-end testing with all major payers.

Results from the end-to-end testing of the revenue cycle with all major payers, including stakeholders, will be one set of predictors for measuring the impact on KPIs established by the risk management team. By continually monitoring their KPIs, organizations can focus on any delays or interruption of cash flow in accounts receivable to contain or avoid them.

THE ROLE OF LCDS IN PREPARING FOR ICD-10

While preparing for ICD-10 transition, healthcare organizations must not overlook the review of LCDs or Local Coverage Determinations. This allows identification of potential areas of concern that may impact the organization. Regional MACs or Medicare Administrative Contractors publish LCDs, outlining the coverage and documentation requirements for specific topics. Such documents enumerate where medical necessity may create potential concerns and how the MAC will approach ICD-10 from a coding perspective.

In general, reimbursement is applicable for claim forms that have a diagnosis code listed as supporting medical necessity. By following coding guidelines, the organization presenting the claim form is accurately representing the medical condition of the patient as documented in their records for the service they are reporting.

However, LCDs provide more information, valuable to both the coding and billing staff and the providers, rather than simply a list of diagnosis codes. Each LCD also provides information on the documentation requirements as well as the source documents used for the guidelines. This allows providers to know exactly what is to be documented to demonstrate medical necessity for a specific study or procedure.

Moreover, LCDs allow providers to evaluate the timeliness of the standards of practice they are using to determine the guidelines. For example, a provider may strongly disagree with an LCD, thereby taking up the first steps towards revision of an outdated LCD. If a MAC decides they will revise something more than only the ICD-10 codes, they will be following the normal processes for LCD development as outlined in the Medicare Program Integrity Manual.

CMS does not expect all contractors will follow a specific process when finalizing revised or new LCDs. As part of the finalization process, contractors are required to post responses to comments received along with a summary of the comments.

CONCLUSION

Healthcare organizations will require undergoing several changes when implementing ICD-10 for meaningful use of Electronic Health Records. Among them, revision of LCDs will definitely be a game-changer and it will impact several organizations. Timely identification of areas of concern and attending to them proactively can potentially avoid extra work, denials and loss of revenue after the implementation date of ICD-10.

<u>REFERENCES</u>

1. Electronic Health Records http://www.himss.org/library/ehr/

2. The "Meaningful Use" Regulation for Electronic Health Records http://www.nejm.org/doi/full/10.1056/nejmp1006114

3. Use of Electronic Health Records in U.S. Hospitals http://www.nejm.org/doi/full/10.1056/nejmsa0900592

4. More physicians and hospitals are using EHRs than before http://www.hhs.gov/news/press/2014pres/08/20140807a.html

HOW ATTACKERS ACHIEVE PERMANENT BACKDOORING OF HTML5 CLIENT-SIDE APPLICATIONS AND AFFECT YOUR SECURITY

WHAT IS PERMANENT BACKDOORING OF HTML5 CLIENT-SIDE APPLICATIONS?

Websites improve the performance of mobile users by using the HTML5 local storage and caching app logic on the client devices. For example, many websites embed third-party widgets, which are a security risk for companies that use such services. Attackers may exploit such local storage caches to create permanent backdoors in these applications.

WHAT HAPPENS IF A CLIENT-SIDE APPLICATION IS EXPLOITED?

Local storage is a common feature of HTML5, and classified as such. It offers a method of saving content on the device of the visitor, and affords more flexibility and larger space than some of the earlier methods such as cookies. Such local storage offers additional benefits to the server, that of code caching.

As web pages routinely require larger blocks of JavaScript, they avoid downloading the code each time the visitor returns to the site. Instead, they save a copy on the local storage of the user. This provides a significant performance boost for a mobile user, who is limited by bandwidth and for whom cookies may not be as useful.

For the attacker, this method has opened new possibilities for compromising the local storage. By injecting a malicious code into the local storage, they open a backdoor that remains on the client-side cache or is persistent. Every time the user visits the site and executes the app, the code delivers its payload and is not affected by closing the browser. Detecting the attack is usually difficult, as the user may not even be aware of anything mischievous happening.

Some advertisements offer a "like" button similar to those on social networking sites such as Facebook and Twitter. This is one of the ways for malicious JavaScript code to transfer itself from the infected site to a user's local storage. Selecting the "like" button on a web page transfers the third-party JavaScript code on the page to the user's local storage. Since the code has the same capabilities as other scripts on the page, the attacker can very easily transfer a malicious code such as XSS into the local storage.

With the resident code in place, an attacker has complete control over the web client. He can access the web application acting as if he were the attacked user, in short, impersonate the user. The attacker now controls all web traffic (to and from) between the user and the web application. The server has no way of recognizing the attack, and even if it did, it has no way of informing the user.

The exploit can have countless different attack payloads. Some of the more common payloads are:

- Stealing session cookies;
- Inducing the user to give up their credentials;
- Injecting Trojans into the system;

- Stealing data such as from the autocomplete cache and

- Logging keystrokes

IS THERE ANY PROTECTION AGAINST SUCH ATTACKS?

The major problem with this is sort of attack is it is not caused by avulnerability, but by a feature that brings convenience. Preventing such attacks is possible through protecting the web pages against manipulation of XSS vulnerability and malicious advertisements. Although this is good enough for the server side, the client side needs more considerations.

To be on the safe side, do not use any user-controlled parameters until you have checked them for malicious content.. If you must, accept only those that you know are safe, whitelist them and black-list all others.

If you are already infected, the following steps will likely provide a solution:

- Close all browser windows leaving only one open;

- Close all tabs in the open window leaving only one;

- In this open tab, call about:blank;

- Delete all data the web application may have stored, including cookies, caches, etc.;

- Restart the browser;

- Alternately, delete the profile of the browser.

REFERENCES:

1. Tyson, J., Gemini Security Solutions, *How a Platform Using HTML5 Can Affect the Security of Your Website.* Available from: <http://securitymusings.com/article/3159/how-a-platform-using-html5-can-affect-the-security-of-your-website>. [1 February 2012].

2. Eilers, C, CtoVision, *HTML5 Security: Learn more about two of many new attacks.* Available from: <http://ctovision.com/2013/04/learn-more-about-two-of-many-new-attacks-html5-security/>. [29 April 2013].

3. Anley, C., The Web Application, *Chapter 2 – Core Defense Mechanisms.* Available from: <http://mdsec.net/wahh/answers2e.html>. [2011].

LAUNCHING THE CLINICAL QUALITY FRAMEWORK & HEALTH EDECISION INITIA- TIVE CLOSE-OUT

Increasing efficiency while improving health and healthcare is paramount and for that the key parts are measuring and improving quality.

Within the S&I or Standards Interoperability framework, the HeD or Health eDecisions project has been leading the charge in accelerating standards for supporting the clinical decision support.

Although the HeD initiative came to a close on March 27, it is only the beginning of their quality efforts and not the end. A new initiative, the CQF or Clinical Quality Framework has been launched in collaboration with CMS or Centers for Medicare and Medicaid Services.

This new collaborative initiative, CQF, will use the work done by the HeD project as its foundation, and will be focusing on harmonizing the standards for electronic clinical quality measurement and clinical decision support. The HeD initiative has already done incredible work for the standards community, and some of their significant achievements are highlighted here.

ACHIEVEMENTS OF THE HED INITIATIVE

Launched in June 2012, the Health eDecision Initiative was handled by a dedicated, passionate and well-organized community. It achieved significant progress in harmonizing standards for CDS or Clinical Decision Support. It took the HeD community less than two years for completing work on two Use Cases:

CDS Artifact Sharing – This Use Case solved the dilemma of sharing a good clinical decision support rule with others via an electronic format, such that they are able to use the rule in their electronic health record.

CDS Guidance Service – This Use Case solved the technical difficulty of sending important data to an up to date service or website that provides advice on immunizations or other decisions of complex nature.

Although it sounds simple enough, this work was no small feat considering how difficult it is to develop standards or the challenges to be faced to get national consensus on standards. Not only did the HeD community evaluate and harmonize standards for Clinical Decision Support, they authored six HL7 standards with the help of the HL7 Work Group of the CDS and created three implementation guides. HL7 is ready to use and test all the standards and implementation guides as "draft standards". Among these standards are the:

1. Implementation Guide for Clinical Decision Support knowledge Artifact

2. Implementation Guide for Decision Support Service

3. Standard for DSS or Decision Support Service

4. Templates for vMR or Virtual Medical Record

5. Specification for vMR XML

6. Logical Model for vMR

The two Implementation Guides have already been included in the proposed notice published in the Federal Register, as appearing in the 2015 Edition NPRM. The HeD team also coordinated pilots of both the Use Cases with various vendors and content providers. After this, they also held the first ever Virtual Open House for S&I Pilots.

Clinical Decision Support is the representation of clinical guidance facing the user. For effective intervention of CDS, it is necessary that there is person-specific data, availability of computable biomedical knowledge and an inference or reasoning mechanism to combine these elements for generating and presenting actionable and helpful information to individuals, clinicians or caregivers in the proper way and at the proper time.

So that these benefits can be optimized, CDS interventions must be more easily implementable and shareable, such that any organization can easily acquire and deploy the interventions. For this, advanced standards are necessary to enable either the regular or the routine consumption of CDS intervention via a web service or by repeatedly importing and updating the CDS artifacts into CDS systems.

Another first, the Virtual Closing Ceremony of the S&I Initiative on March 27 honored those who participated in the initiative as an appreciation for all the hard work done by the community. The virtual closing ceremony included a review of the accomplishments of the initiative, insights from the participants of the HeD initiative and shared the "real world" applications of their work.

ANALYTICS AND DATA MINING IN HEALTHCARE

ANALYTICS AND DATA MINING IN HEALTHCARE

Statistically speaking, mining of big data and its analytics in healthcare is evolving very fast, while providing insight from extremely large data sets. Although this has huge potential and is already helping to improve outcomes with reduced costs, several challenges still need to be overcome.

Patient care, compliance and regulatory requirements bind the healthcare industry, which has a history of keeping records and in the process, generates a huge amount of data. Traditionally, they store it mostly in hard copy form on paper and film, but the current trend in the healthcare industry is to digitize these massive quantities of data rapidly.

Pressure on the industry to improve its healthcare delivery at reduced costs and comply with mandatory requirements is forcing it to consider the potential of big data, as the vast quantities of data are currently known. The industry is discovering the hidden potential of big data, which includes among others, population health management, disease surveillance and clinical decision support.

A very rudimentary idea of the humongous size comes from reports stating that big data from US healthcare is rapidly approaching the zettabyte scale and will very soon enter the yottabyte. A zettabyte equals 10^{21}GB and one yottabyte is 10^{24}GB. A California-based health network alone is reported to have about 40 petabytes (40x 1,048,576GB) of such data from EHRs.

Common data management tools and traditional methods are woefully inadequate to deal with big data. Even traditional hardware and software finds it difficult to handle the extremely large and complex electronic health data sets that the healthcare industries churn out. Apart from its sheer volume, two aspects make healthcare big data such a daunting prospect – diversity of data types and the speed of handling.

Simply stated, big data in the healthcare industry is made up of information from patient healthcare and well-being. This includes inputs from CPOE and clinical decision support systems, EPRs or electronic patient records, machine generated or sensor data, social media posts and updates, blogs and web pages, data from emergency care, news feeds and articles belonging to medical journals.

Amidst this vast array and amount of data, there is a huge opportunity of discovering associations while understanding the underlying trends and patterns. Big data analytics has the potential to lower costs, save lives and improve health care. The industry can use big data to extract insights leading to better-informed decisions.

New critical factors such as meaningful use and pay for performance are emerging in today's healthcare environment, changing the reimbursement model. Healthcare organizations need to acquire proper tools, infrastructure and techniques for taking effective advantage of big data to prevent potential loss of millions of dollars in revenue and profit.

DATA MINING CHALLENGES IN HEALTHCARE

The $3-trillion US healthcare Industry expects use of big data will improve patient outcomes, make the system more transparent and lead to a more accessible and affordable care. According to the Health Data Consortium, the ability to anticipate and treat illnesses increases manifolds with the power to access and analyze big data. On one hand, this data helps in recognizing individuals at risk related to serious health problems. On the other, it can identify waste in the system as well as lower the cost of healthcare across the board.

Before delivering major insights, companies owning the analytics engines require access to the necessary information. Hospitals, primary care providers, researchers, health insurers, state and federal governments among others hold a staggering amount of healthcare data. The problem – each of these acts as a silo, with only a little transparency across them.

Among the aggregation of massive amounts of data, looms the challenge of maintaining patient privacy. Although the success of big data will not mean private data becomes public, healthcare will have to figure out how to leverage the information for delivering better quality patient care, while keeping the information secure.

A major driving force behind the momentum came from the Affordable Care Act. It incentivized providers to become more data-driven and to facilitate data sharing. Increased sharing will make the entire healthcare system more transparent. For example, big data is proving critical in measuring the success of ACOs or Accountable Care Organizations. However, coordination, collection and analysis of huge amounts of data and implementation of the findings are as yet years down the road.

ANALYTICS AND HEALTH INFORMATICS

Currently, health informatics is entering a new era, where technology is starting to handle big data. This is opening up huge opportunities in data mining and big data analytics helping to realize the goals of diagnosing, treating, helping and healing patients in need. The ultimate goal of this industry is to improve the quality of care that it can provide to end users, that is, improving the domain of HCO or Health Care Output.

Combining computer science and information science within the realm of healthcare produces health informatics. Currently a lot of research is underway within this field including bioinformatics, image informatics, clinical informatics, public health informatics and translational bioinformatics. Research in health informatics covers data acquisition, retrieval, storage and analytics by employing data mining techniques.

Attempts are made to define big data to make it easier to incorporate in various studies. One way of defining big data is by using five V's – Value, Veracity, Variety, Velocity and Volume. While Value defines the quality of data in reference to intended results, Veracity measures how genuine the data is. Where Variety defines the level of complexity, Velocity is the pace at which new data is generated, while Volume points to the physical amount of this data.

Health informatics research uses data that has many of the above stated qualities. Since the basic goal is to improve HCO, most data inherently has high value. Apart from data collected by traditional methods such as in a clinic, which is essentially regarded as being high in value, data gathered from social media may also be regarded as high value.

Data coming from faulty clinical sensors, gene microarray or even from patient information stored in databases may be erroneous, incomplete or noisy. This may be a cause for concern when Health informatics deals with data that requires high veracity. It may be necessary to evaluate such data properly before dealing with it.

Healthcare generates different types of data. For example, search query data may come from different age groups or a complex database. Health informatics has to see this big variety at many levels since there may be a large quantity of varying types of independent attributes.

With new data coming in at increasing speeds, health informatics has to deal with big velocity. Real-time monitoring of events are a common generator for such data, for example, medical sensors tracking or monitoring the current condition of a patient or a multitude of incoming web posts giving the latest situation in an unfolding epidemic.

Big data has huge volumes coming from the large amounts of records hospitals store for patients. Some instances can be quite large, such as when datasets are generated for gene microarray or MRI images for each patient. On the other hand, social media data collected from a large population may also constitute a large pool.

Although defining or classifying big data with the five qualities does not cover all the types encountered by health informatics, most impose significant procedural constraints and require some way of addressing. For example, EHRs may be difficult to store in offline storages because of their high volume, even when not exhibiting big velocity or variety. Real-time continuous data may require very high-throughput processing because of its high velocity, even though it is not big in volume. Big value data without big veracity may require complex methods of adjustment such as expanding the size of the dataset. That means definitions of big data that merely focus on volume and velocity may actually not be considering enough qualities of the dataset to characterize it fully.

Although a lot of research is eventually helping answer events in the clinical realm, in reality, there exists a gap of about 13-17 years between clinical research and actual clinical care hospitals use in practice. Most decisions made these days depend on general information that has worked before. With the explosion of big data and the research in health informatics, healthcare systems will be able to garner new ways of being more accurate, reliable and efficient.

Health informatics gains medical insight from applying analytics and data mining to population data as well. This data may be gathered from experts or hospitals in the traditional form or from social media. Either way, this data has big volume, big velocity and big variety, but possibly low veracity and low value. However, depending on the techniques used for extracting useful information, this type of data may also have big value.

CONCLUSION

Health informatics comprising analytics and data mining in healthcare shows tremendous promise while providing inspiration for the future courses of action. It shows the importance of using all accessible levels of data to advantage. As computational power increases, methods more efficient and accurate will be developed, leading to newer levels of human existence.

REFERENCES

1. What is Data Mining in Healthcare? https://www.health-catalyst.com/data-mining-in-healthcare

2. A review of data mining using big data in health informatics http://www.journalofbigdata.com/content/1/1/2

3. Big data analytics in healthcare: promise and potential http://www.hissjournal.com/content/2/1/3

4. How Big Data Will Help Save Healthcare http://www.forbes.com/sites/castlight/2014/11/10/how-big-data-will-help-save-healthcare

HOW DOES NETWORK AUTOMATION BRING NETWORKING AND SECURITY TOGETHER?

WHAT IS NETWORK AUTOMATION?

With network automation, an organization improves the availability of its network services. The phrase fundamentally describes the processes, methods, and technologies used in enterprises and large organizations to configure and manage their network devices such as the hubs, routers and switches.

In the past decade, there has been an explosion of increasingly complex network devices. In addition, with the adoption of BYOD policies, cloud services, virtualization, and mobile working practices, the challenges faced by the modern network has increased exponentially. .

An example would be in order here. Only a few years ago, one needed to punch a hole in the single firewall to let a new service request through. Today, the same request requires a change in several layers of security, changes in ACL rules and in multiple firewalls, switches and integrated routers. The introduction of multiple vendors further complicates the issue.

Classically, in an enterprise, the security teams are responsible for the firewalls and the network teams are responsible for the routers and switches. The roles of the two teams have always been clearly defined. However, with the networks becoming larger, broader, and more complex, both the teams have to work more closely and collaborate.

THE PROBLEMS IN BRINGING NETWORKING AND SECURITY TOGETHER

Although collaboration is beneficial, there is a downside to it. The security and the networking teams have specified experience and knowledge in their own domains. They are unlikely to be able to carry out the tasks required by the other team, and this may involve a significant risk of creating errors.

For example, members of the networking team are not likely to be familiar with the different nuances and subtleties of syntax used by various vendors. Likewise, the security teams are more adept at setting internal policies governing the best practices of the enterprise, and this can impact the networking team.

If one team does not have the expertise to perform the tasks of the other team, frustrations and challenges can quickly grow and affect the overall functioning of the enterprise.

HOW DOES NETWORK AUTOMATION HELP?

With automation, a high volume of required changes can be analyzed by the security team, tested, and provisioned across the network, saving considerable amount of time. Automation takes care of the different rules and syntax required for separate devices and vendors, which is the major consumer of time in such cases.

With automation, network teams are able to make changes in firewall policies as required in one place and distribute these changes across the network quickly, with automation taking care of the multi-vendor devices. This reduces the time and effort required for the deployment, and eliminates the need to make changes to individual devices.

HOW DOES NETWORK AUTOMATION INCREASE EFFICIENCY?

Network automation provides a holistic, automated approach over the entire network management. It extends over the domain of fault, performance, availability, configuration, change, compliance, and process automation. The key benefits can be listed as:

- Cost reduction by automating manual compliance and configuration tasks;

- Audit and compliance requirements pass easily with audit and compliance reports and proactive policy deployments;

- Improvement in network security by the recognition and fixing of vulnerabilities before they impact the network;

- Increase in network uptime and availability by preventing mis-configurations and inconsistencies;

- Application integrations are delivered by process-powered automation, delivering full IT lifecycle workflow automation.

REFERENCES:

1. Search Networking, *Network automation tools: Should you build or buy?* Available from: <http://searchnet-working.techtarget.com/Network-automation-tools-Should-you-build-or-buy>. [Oct 2013].

2. Pao, P., Hewlett Packard, *Efficient change, automated configuration & secure compliance.* Available from: <http://www8.hp.com/us/en/software-solutions/soft-ware.html?compURI=1169982#.Ud6GzeEu18M>. [2013].

3. Nye, S., Help Net Security, *Bringing networking and security together through network automation.* Available from: <http://www.net-security.org/article.php?id=1837>. [10 May 2013].

HUMAN ERROR & PATIENT DATA SECURITY THREATS

The greatest threat of a healthcare data breach is from employee negligence.

The fourth annual Patient Privacy and Data Security Study conducted by the Ponemon Institute substantiated some facts about healthcare data breach that were already known. The study reviewed some new and expanded threats relating to patient data security and privacy. Of the 91 healthcare organizations who participated in this study, they concluded that more than 75 percent of the organizations view negligence from employees as the greatest threat to data breach, and that human error remains the biggest source of breaches for healthcare data.

SIGNIFICANT FINDINGS OF THE REPORT

Ponemon conducted their research by interviewing 388 healthcare providers. A total of 91 healthcare organizations were involved and, which is 11 more than their sample size in 2012. Some topics covered in the study include:

- The need to reduce internal as well as external threats
- HIPAA compliance trends

- Cloud security
- Mobile device security

Following negligence, 41 percent of the participating organizations noted their biggest security concern were the use of public cloud services, 40 percent listed mobile device insecurity and 39 percent were insecure over cyber-attacks.

An astounding figure of 90 percent of the respondents in the study confirmed they have had at least one data breach within the last two years. Of that 90 percent, 38 percent confirmed having more than five data breaches over the same two-year period; last year this figure was 45 percent. According to the study, the only positive result favorable to the healthcare industry is that data breach cost and frequency has declined slightly over the past one year as compared to the previous years. The chairman and founder of the Ponemon Institute, Larry Ponemon, concluded that this was an indication that organizations are making modest but good progress in managing sensitive patient data.

The primary causes of breaches were as follows:

- Computing devices, lost or stolen – 49 percent
- Unintentional actions or mistakes by employees – 46 percent
- Snafus from third-parties – 41 percent

Assessing it in economic terms, the study reported that data breaches had cost the healthcare organizations between less than $10,000 to more than $1 million. As calculated by Ponemon, the average monetary impact of data breaches is in the $2 million range over a two year period, for the healthcare organizations represented in the study. Compared to last year, this is actually down from 2.4 million. The figure is down partly because of the decrease in the size of the breaches, since the average number of stolen or lost records per breach came down to 2,150; it was 3,000 records earlier. Ponemon estimates $188 per record, which makes the cost of one breach $404,200.

Of the critical themes mentioned in the report, three of them were HIPAA compliance, cloud security and mobile security. The report claims that nearly 88 percent of the healthcare organizations allow their medical staff and employees to bring and use their own devices (BYOD). However, over half of the organizations are not confident of the security of these personally owned mobile devices.

Furthermore, only 23 percent of the organizations confirmed that they insist on anti-malware/anti-virus software being resident on the mobile device before it is connected to their network. Only 22 percent require that mobile devices be scanned for viruses and malware before connection, and only 14 percent want removal of all mobile applications that present a security threat. Healthcare organizations have started to realize that with more tablets and smartphones now being used in the workplace, one of the greatest sources of data breach is the loss of devices.

The use of cloud for backup and storage, file sharing applications, document sharing and collaboration and business applications has increased to 40 percent; the figure was 32 percent last year. However, only one third expressed having any real confidence over the security of information stored in a public cloud environment.

While only 49 percent of the respondents said they are either not compliant or only partially compliant with HIPAA, 51 percent confirmed they are fully compliant with HIPAA requirements. Moreover, 39 percent said that their incident assessment process is non-effective primarily due to lack of consistency and their inability to scale their processes.

Only 33 percent were somewhat confident and 40 percent were not confident at all that their business associates had the capability to detect, perform an incident risk assessment and notify the organization in the event of an information breach incident, as required under the BAA or business associate agreement. While 44 percent of the healthcare organizations say the HIPAA Omnibus Rule has affected their programs, 41 percent claim no change and 15 percent are yet undecided.

Some entities covered by HIPAA and HITECH are adopting a strategy of trying to be just compliant without caring for the broader, cross-industry security risks. However, organizations are learning that compliance with HIPAA does not necessarily translate into good security for the organization.

Organizations are striving to achieve the requirements of HHS or OCR, whether it is through better procedures, policies or training. However, they are missing the boat because healthcare ecosystems are increasingly becoming more complex and this is evident in several recent incidents. It is not enough to rely on telling an employee that they are responsible for PHI protection, necessary technologies and tools must be in place. For example, encryption makes it less likely for an employee to do anything to protect the data.

SOME OTHER KEY FINDINGS

Of the healthcare organizations represented in the report, 69 percent believe that ACA increases the risk to patient privacy and security significantly. Primary concerns were, 75 percent worried about insecure exchange of patient information between healthcare providers and government, 65 percent cite the risk to be patient data on insecure databases and 63 percent on patient registration on insecure websites.

While 51 percent of the organizations are part of an ACO or Accountable Care Organization, 66 percent say the risk to patient security and privacy has increased because of an increase in the exchange of patient health information among participants.

Only 32 percent of the respondents are confident about the security and privacy of patient data being shared on HIEs, while 40 percent are not confident at all.

Only 25 percent of the respondents or less than half of the organizations in the study confirmed they are fully compliant with the AOD or Accounting of Disclosure requirement; 23 percent are nearly in full compliance.

Almost all respondents deemed that medical files, insurance records and billing records are the ones most likely to be lost or stolen.

THIRD PLATFORM TECHNOLOGIES IN HEALTHCARE

THIRD PLATFORM TECHNOLOGIES IN HEALTHCARE

The IT industry started with first platform behemoths such as the mainframes, which later gave way to the second platform, the client/servers that came into prominence with the proliferation of desktop computers. Currently, the IT industry is thriving on the third platform of computing, namely, cloud computing, mobiles, big data and the social networks. This is a much bigger influencer of the IT world as compared to the first and second platforms ever were. Not only the IT industry, anyone doing business in today's world is affected, and that includes the healthcare industry as well.

Therefore, very little additional investment is going towards the legacy IT infrastructure – the first and second platforms. While the major investments are moving towards the third platform, industry is utilizing some of this investment to rip out the existing legacy environment and replacing it with SaaS or Software as a Service.

While the strategic issue for enterprise IT users is how to quickly reorient their budgets, for third-platform providers, the issue is how to quickly meet the critical demands of enterprise IT in identifying, selecting, learning and implementing new platforms. For both, rapid reskilling is an urgent necessity – leading to a huge employee churn as everyone adjusts to the reality of this new infrastructure.

THE STRONGLY GROWING PUBLIC CLOUD

According to IDC, the private vs. public cloud computing war is decisively leaning towards public cloud computing. IDC predicts that the share of public CSPs or Could Service Providers will be a full 75% of the total investment in cloud use in the near future and increase thereafter.

The imbalance between the spending on private and public growth has occurred due to the massive growth in the demand for public cloud adoption. Not many are willing to spend on internal private environments, given that operating with public cloud is getting more secure and less expensive. According to IDC, this imbalance is going to be even more pronounced in 2015 and beyond.

This dramatic shift towards public cloud computing is affecting the server market as well. A majority of server shipments, including those from ODMs, is going towards datacenters of cloud service providers, and this is expected to grow further. This also means that server companies are increasingly focusing their new designs on the requirements of CSPs.

OFFERING HEALTHCARE IT AS A SERVICE

According to a joint report from MeriTalk and EMC, healthcare providers will save money in the long run by adopting cloud technology, analytics, mobile and social media. They could even use their EHR systems as a service. This is likely to happen soon, as IT leaders try to bring the SMAC stack or Social, Mobile, Analytics and Cloud technology together into a single, integrated architecture.

With this type of architecture, healthcare can easily catch up to other verticals in the industry. With SMAC, hospitals can demonstrate a return on investment in EHR or electronic health record systems. Moving beyond meaningful use, hospitals can offer IT as a service leveraging it both within and outside its walls.

Healthcare providers are increasingly turning towards SMAC stack, referring to the collective technology or the third platform as Futurecare. For example, many ambulatory providers are increasingly using cloud EHR; increased use of common analytics is reducing risk analysis and readmissions; providers are increasingly using mobile health to view patient information, receiving clinical information and filling electronic prescriptions; social technology is increasingly helping to improve communication among physicians and with patients.

Each type of technology component within the SMAC stack supports a different step in the management of population health. For example, the use of cloud offers access, use of big data offers identification, using mobility enables engagement between physicians and patients, while social technology triggers perpetual activation. This is one way healthcare CIOs should think of their EHR systems – as providing IT as a service. This will allow them to exhibit ROI even after meeting meaningful use.

THE THIRD PLATFORM AND INFORMATION TO PATIENTS

Since the passage of healthcare reform legislation in 2010, the implementation of electronic records and technologies and the offer of incentives from the government for meaningful uses or IT, the healthcare industry in the US are currently going through a rapid transformation. A greater collaboration between providers and payers can be expected as these changes reflect increasingly in business models. The erstwhile fee-for-service model is slowly giving way to fee-for-value incentives.

The third platform and its components, SMAC, are playing a decisive role in this alteration. Healthcare is taking advantage of cloud-based portals using industry-specific solutions. Analytics and mobile solutions are proving effective in removing surprises from the process, and for tightening patient engagement. Healthcare as a whole is moving towards a goal of reducing costs, while simultaneously improving the quality of care and outcomes.

If there are sudden health issues, such as accidents and emergencies including serious ones, the present healthcare industry can take care very well. It has also done wonders in the field of public health. However, healthcare faces the maximum cost challenge when treating chronic conditions. This is mostly related to the aging population that is living longer.

With inappropriate technology, it becomes an expensive and difficult proposition to treat the previously mentioned conditions. However, with solutions from the third platform, things are changing for the better.

In the US, some mobile service providers are pursuing an innovative initiative wherein they offer customers advertising services with greater personalization and relevance. Such offers in the third platform can engage patients by offering them information helping them to make the best choice about key health-related decisions.

Healthcare providers are increasingly using predictive analytics supported by cloud, social, mobile and big data services to use education, social influence and even sending reminders to patients, thereby helping to change their behavior.

Healthcare providers have always found providing individualized care to be an expensive proposition. This was mostly because their staff had to manage the regime of each patient individually. With the third platform technologies, the process can be automated and made cost-effective. Moreover, proactive care, such as prenatal information services, can be easily provided with regimens tailored to the needs of the individual. Today, most healthcare systems and private payers are trying to manage the health of the population by experimenting with these technologies.

WHAT HEALTHCARE SHOULD LOOK FOR WHEN IMPLEMENTING THIRD PLATFORM

According to IDC, there are some important factors to be taken care of when the healthcare industry takes the initiative of using third platform solutions. These new digital transformation initiatives may also be considered as best practices.

Refreshing Competence In IT – Third platform solutions require skills significantly different from what was necessary for first and second platforms. Social technologies, mobile, big data and cloud require a fresh look at the new technologies and business practices. Healthcare needs to focus more on their core competence by becoming leaner and outsourcing more of their non-core activities.

Rethinking The Basic Business Model – The third platform takes the existing business model and stands it on its head. Not only does it touch upon the organizational core business model, but makes drastic changes that extend well beyond the IT organization. The new digital transformation initiatives lead the organization to debate on whether to continue with the old model or to leverage the innovations provided by the third platform.

For example, the old model had all the important assets behind firewalls while the organization worked with only a few partners. The third platform would enable the hospital to work with a community of potential partners to leverage their core IP. Healthcare organizations could then have the option to enable new business models, such as allowing amplification of values by using cloud services for distributing their products and services. This would also enable partners deliver value-added services by themselves.

Leveraging Cloud Platforms – With mushrooming industry-specific cloud platforms, healthcare industry has the option of leveraging the new generation of third platform solutions that suit its specific industrial needs. New services are coming up that offer levels of value going well beyond the legacy horizontal core business systems such as CRM or ERP. Healthcare industry would do well to take advantage of these new services as early as possible.

Being an Industry-Specific Platform Provider – Hospitals can move beyond merely using industry-specific cloud platforms to becoming industry-specific platform providers. This is a tremendous opportunity to transform their business. For example, hospitals can use the cloud as a place to market and distribute their intellectual property content while using the platform for enabling a community of innovative players who can create, market and distribute their own services.

That allows the hospital to become the center of innovation in the industry while enabling others to distribute content through their portal. This helps the hospital to increase its visibility and viability within the industry.

Using Pre-Integrated Solutions For Industry Digitization – Today, vendors offer a variety of approaches supporting transformation to a digital enterprise. This encompasses the entire field of clouds, mobile, social and analytic solutions including a new generation of finely focused point solutions. These can fast-track the digitization of critical and fast-evolving processes.

Revamping The Intelligent Infrastructure, Customer Analytics and Digital Commerce – By implementing the third platform solutions, the healthcare industry can use a wide variety of initiatives for digital transformation. This includes new ways in which companies reach out to customers, learn about their preferences and behavior, while at the same time, develop innovations.

Finding Suitable Partners – One of the important components of the third platform is that instead of trying to do everything by themselves, healthcare organizations must outsource their non-core activities. That will allow them to focus on their core competence while taking advantage of their partners' expertise in accelerating their journey towards innovation and growth. Partners must be able to provide world-class competence in third platform solutions and have the best practices and acumen for business consulting to help in the transition.

CONCLUSION

Healthcare organizations planning to embark on a journey on the third platform must not shirk from reinventing themselves. Not only will this help them become the IT organization of the third platform, they should also try to become the enterprises of the third platform. The transformation to the third platform has already started and those not considering moving forward now may find the competition is leaving them behind.

REFERENCES

Exploring Enterprise IT Transformation During the Transition to "Third Platform" Technologies http://enterprise.huawei.com/en/about/e-journal/ict/detail/hw-275497.htm

As IDC Sees It, Tech's 'Third Platform' Disrupts Everyone http://www.cio.com/article/2377568/cloud-computing/as-idc-sees-it-tech-s-third-platform-disrupts-everyone.html

Future Points to Healthcare IT as a Service http://www.cio.com/article/2834834/healthcare/future-points-to-healthcare-it-as-a-service.html

The 3rd Platform: Enabling Digital Transformation http://www.tcs.com/SiteCollectionDocuments/White-Papers/3rd-Platform-Enabling-Digital-Transformation.pdf

CONTROLLING ADMINISTRATIVE PRIVILEGES

WHAT HAPPENS IF ADMINISTRATIVE PRIVILEGES ARE NOT UNDER CONTROL?

One of the primary ways for an attacker to gain entry into an enterprise network is by misusing the administrative privileges. Attackers usually follow one of two methods for gaining access. In the first method, the attacker manages to fool one of the privileged users of a workstation into opening a document from a malicious website, or surf a website hosting malicious content, which automatically exploits the visitor's browser.

The malicious code then runs on the victim's computer, and if the victim user's account has administrative privileges, takes over their computer completely. After this it is relatively simple for the attacker to install sniffers, keystroke loggers, and various remote control software to then dig out administrative passwords thus gaining access to sensitive data. Such attacks are common through e-mails. If an unsuspecting administrator were to open an e-mail containing an infected attachment, the attacker gains access to the system using this as a pivot point to attack other systems.

Attackers may also gain access by a secondary method: guessing or cracking a password used by an administrator. This gives the attacker access to the target machine.

With administrative privileges distributed widely and loosely, the attacker's work of compromising these privileges is made easier since so many other accounts are now available.

HOW DOES THIS AFFECT THE ENTERPRISE?

An administrator has absolute privileges over the entire enterprise network. If the attacker were able to elevate his privileges equal to the level of an administrator, then he could masquerade as the administrator himself and quickly gain control over all the resources in the network.

This allows the attacker to inflict major damage to the enterprise by stealing or modifying confidential data, disrupting daily operating procedures, upsetting financial transactions, slowing down network traffic, denying legitimate service to other users and diverting communication and sensitive data to offsite malicious servers.

WHAT IS THE BEST WAY TO MITIGATE THIS THREAT?

Use administrative privileges only when necessary. Introduce focused auditing on all persons who use the administrative privileges and monitor all anomalous behavior. Inventory all the administrative privileges using an automated tool, and validate that a senior executive has authorized each person who uses administrative privileges.

Change over all administrative passwords to be complex formations of intermixed special characters, numbers, letters and alphabets. Strong passwords of sufficient length make it difficult for the attacker to guess and to crack.

Passwords for administrators should be changed at frequent intervals. Any new device, when being introduced to the networked environment, must have all its default passwords changed to longer and relatively more difficult passwords.

Passwords for all systems must be stored in an encrypted format, only readable by those with super-user privileges. The control lists must ensure that administrative accounts are used only for activities requiring system administration and not for general activities such as reading e-mails.

REFERENCES:

1. The SANS Institute, *Critical Control 12: Controlled Use of Administrative Privileges.* Available from: <http://www.sans.org/critical-security-controls/control.php?id=12>. [2013].

2. Hau, D., The SANS Institute, *Unauthorized Access – Threats, Risk, and Control.* Available from: <http://www.giac.org/paper/gsec/3161/unauthorized-access-threats-risk-control/105264>. [11 July 2013].

3. Computer Economica, *Security Threats in Employee Misuse of IT Resources.* Available from: <http://www.computereconomics.com/article.cfm?id=1436>. [March 2009].

TEXT MESSAGING COMPLIANCE & HIPAA

Although sending unencrypted text messages involves significant risks of noncompliance with HIPAA and other acts, the method is a fast and convenient way to communicate.

There can be significant risks involved with transmitting Electronic Protected Health Information or ePHI using unencrypted text messaging, especially with the increasing pressure of enforcing the compliance with HITECH and HIPAA. On the other hand, healthcare providers see text messaging as a fast and convenient way to collaborate and communicate with colleagues.

THE COMPLIANCE MANDATE OF HIPAA AND HITECH

According to the HIPAA Security Rule, organizations must address text messaging as a part of their management strategy and carry out a comprehensive risk analysis. Depending on the outcome of the risk analysis, the organization must decide on the appropriate technical, physical and administrative controls that will mitigate the risks of using text messaging for sending ePHI.

Before the healthcare organization can decide on the necessary technical security measures that it requires for complying with this standard, it must review the current methods it is using for transmitting ePHI. As a next step, it has to identify the means available as well as appropriate for protecting ePHI and select a suitable solution. The healthcare organization can send adequately protected ePHI an over open, electronic network, without violating the Security Rule.

HITECH requires healthcare organizations to notify patients in cases of breach of ePHI. Texting impacts this area of compliance as well. The HIPAA Final Rule defines "breach" as the disclosure, use, access or acquisition of PHI in a manner not permitted by the HIPAA Privacy Rule, which compromises the privacy or security of such information.

Typically, texting involves use of devices such as tablets and smartphones and these can potentially be lost or stolen. Therefore, it is important that healthcare organizations review and ensure HITECH compliance in the event of a breach when the text message resides on such a compromised device.

POLICY SHOULD INCLUDE TEXT MESSAGING

Use of text messaging must be a part of the policy of the healthcare organization. Effectively, the scope should include all employees, physicians and affiliates. In addition, a Business Associate Agreement or BAA may be required for including third parties such as vendors and contractors to abide by parts of the policy of the organization. Moreover, the policy must cover all applications, systems and networks that process, store or transmit ePHI and other sensitive information.

For establishing the minimal requirements in the organization, its policy for secure text messaging should include key statements such as:

- Text messages are electronic communications. A computer or a mobile device may be used to transmit text messages, which may include written words, videos and photos. When the content of such a message contains ePHI, the text message must comply with HIPAA requirements.

- Only an approved, encrypted and secure format must be used for transmitting any text message containing ePHI.

REQUIREMENTS TO BE MET IN THE POLICY

When transmitting, storing or processing ePHI using a text messaging application, certain requirements must be met, such as:

Before sending any text message containing ePHI, users must make sure that the application will encrypt the message during both transit and while at rest. The mobile provider or a software program must encrypt the message when sending it from the sending device to the recipient's device. The cellular provider must not store the encrypted or decrypted text message on their systems in ways that it is accessible to an unauthorized person.

When employees wish to send ePHI via text messages to other employees, all senders and receivers must fulfill encryption requirements for messages both in transit and at rest.

Employees sending or receiving text messages containing ePHI, must make sure that they are using a secure text application approved by the IT department as suitable for the purpose. Employees must submit their mobile numbers for a proper inventory to be maintained by the IT department.

It is necessary to properly sanitize any retired mobile device that was used for texting ePHI. The IT department must wipe all mobile devices securely when they are returned. Employees using personal devices must contact the IT department and have their devices securely wiped prior to returning it to their cellular provider.

To be effective, the policy enforcing the use of secure text messaging must mandate safeguards to be implemented by employees who wish to send or receive messages. These safeguards must include:

- Password protection for the mobile device or the secure texting application; the user should never disable this feature.

- Automatic lock enabled after a period of inactivity not exceeding five minutes.

- Limiting to the minimum necessary information when texting messages with ePHI - multiple factors identifying the patient must not be used

To ensure accuracy of the information being texted, some precautions must be administered. The following guidelines must be followed when texting ePHI:

- Before sending, confirm presence of the recipient

- Recipient must confirm reception of the message

- Do not use abbreviations or shorthand

- Be careful about using auto-correction functions; review text for accuracy prior to sending

- Do not text patient orders

- Make sure that all text messages used for clinical decision making are documented in medical records

- If the information is no longer needed, delete all text messages containing ePHI as early as possible

Based on the compliance mandate of specific organizations, policy statements to be considered and adopted may include:

- All unencrypted text messages with ePHI received or sent out must be immediately reported to the IT department or to the HIPAA Security Officer

- Any text message sent to a wrong individual must be reported to the IT department or to the HIPAA Security Officer

- Maintain every revision of a policy and procedure for a minimum period of six years from the date of its creation or when it was last in effect, whichever is later

- Maintain all logs relevant to security incidents and log-in audit information for a period of six years

REQUIREMENTS TO BE MET BY A SECURE TEXTING SOLUTION

For ensuring compliance with HIPAA requirements, and enable employees to use text messaging securely, healthcare organizations must work with vendors that meet the following key capabilities:

Authentication methods: End-to-end secure authentication methods and environment methods must be provided to ensure authorized access

Password management: Generation and use of sufficiently complex passwords along with secure mechanisms for change/reset

Administrator rights: Must be separate from regular user rights

Login monitoring: Must log and monitor all attempts, both successful and failures. Must lock the account after a defined number of failed login attempts

Access control: Users must have access only to the messages they have sent or received Logging of all administrative access and actions including resetting of administrative passwords for users

Automatic logoff: Must log out the user from the application after a period of inactivity

Unique user identification: Users must be uniquely identified throughout the application and it must be possible to tie all actions directly to these IDs

Access control audits: Must be able to generate reports on access controls, including actions of administrators

Account authorization and establishment: Only administrators must have the ability to create new accounts. Must log all account creation and modifications

Account termination: Only an administrator should be able to terminate an account Terminated accounts must not be able to access any previous messages and must not be able to send any new message

Audit capabilities: Must log all user actions related to message actions and authentication, must log all administrative access related to elevated access activities and managing users, must time-stamp all logs for easier correlation

Transmission security: Must ensure that the data is protected while in transit. The transmission security provided must be independent of the transmitting platform

Data protection on the mobile device: Messages stored on mobile devices must be encrypted independent of any native device encryption. All proprietary data cached on the device must also be encrypted. Encryption algorithm must conform to industry standard AES256. Resetting the application password must destroy all saved messages

Backup processes: All messages must be archived for allowing administrative access. Archived messages must be encrypted and stored securely. Third party storage must not have access to archived ePHI. Message retention times must be customizable to meet the requirements of the organizational policy. Access to message archives must be restricted

Cloud-hosted solution: Solution must be a cloud-hosted SaaS that does not require on-premise hardware or infrastructure

Secure photo sharing: Must allow photos to be taken and attached to text messages. Sharing or accessing outside the texting application must not be possible

Texting across multiple organizations: A single application must allow texting across multiple organizations. Users with multiple accounts can have a contact directory and a unified inbox

Notifications and read receipts: Must provide notifications and read receipts as visual indication and time stamp

Callback requests: Must embed phone number directly into the message to enable callback with a single tap

Streamlined contact directory: Must allow users to search, find and text all contacts in the application directory, without typing any phone number. Administrators must be able to populate the contact directory

Customizable sounds: Must allow users to set the tone of the sound alert when a new message is received.

Administrative Requirements to Be Met By a Secure Texting Solution

Active Directory synchronization: Must be able to add/remove/modify users directly. Administrators must be able to setup the synchronization without referring to the vendor

Secure notification: Message notifications displayed must not contain any ePHI

Remote wipe: Administrator must be able to disable accounts, revoking access to all messages and information

Preventing ePHI leakage: Incorrect entry of PIN on the mobile device for a certain number of times must destroy all saved data

Maintain organizational privacy: must not allow third parties to access ePHI

Set message life span: Administrator must be able to set how long messages will persist within an application on the device

Optional application PIN: Administrator must be able to set additional PIN on the application.

THE PRACTICE OF TRACKING AND MONITORING

With the deployment of a secure text messaging solution, ensuring active management is critical for maintaining compliance with HITECH and HIPAA requirements. This includes regular monitoring of log files and audit information for ensuring appropriate use. IT administrators must regularly:

- Track and monitor activities related to managing policies and users

- Ensure that all authentication events are captured appropriately

- Ensure that message read receipts have a time stamp

In addition, healthcare organizations must ensure that their proactive audit practice is aligned with the established policy and is implemented for managing the secure and HIPAA-compliant text-messaging framework.

HOW TO PROTECT AGAINST
WEB ATTACKS

It is extremely difficult for a company, after noticing some unusual financial transactions, to immediately ascertain whether it was an internal fraud or embezzlement or a cyber-crime attack. Attacking a company from the outside and siphoning off funds through, say, fraudulent payroll accounts, is a common form of web attack. Between 2008 and 2010, attackers caused damages worth $3 million in at least 53 Seattle based enterprises, and this is just the tip of the iceberg.

NEVER BE COMPLACENT ABOUT SECURITY

Most companies think their system will hold against cyber-crime, and this complacency leads to their undoing when they find smart and ambitious crooks have breached their security. Careless disposal of old equipment such as old laptops, without proper data wipe-off, is also one of the many ways crooks can gain access to security systems.

Apart from the financial loss and the cost of repairs, being a victim of cyber-crime can cost a business its customers. Tabulus Inc. found in a survey that more than 80% of their respondents preferred to warn others to stop business deals with companies that had suffered a security breach. The survey also found that the same respondents held companies to be more trustworthy if these companies had no history of a security breach.

VULNERABLE WI-FI NETWORKS

Victims of cyber-attack are usually compromised via their unprotected Wi-Fi networks. Attacker gangs outfit their cars with high-powered antennas and drive around, scanning for poorly protected or unlocked networks. Once such a network is found, it is an easy task for the attackers to scour the machines on the network and steal passwords and financial data.

The best possible defense that a company can have against such exploits is to avoid wireless networks and use only wired networks. Wired networks are somewhat more secure because they need a physical connection to access them. If a wireless network is necessary, the service set identifier or SSID broadcasting function must be disabled on the wireless router. This prevents casual Wi-Fi snoops from discovering the now hidden network, as users who know the exact network name can only detect this. For added security, the network's information can be periodically changed and only the genuine users informed of the current network name and passcode.

Many Wi-Fi modems and routers still use the WEP encryption algorithm that is outdated by almost 10 years and is easily cracked by the attackers. This must be updated to the current standard WPA2, which is more difficult to break into.

E-MAILS AND HARMFUL WEBSITES

Attacks from spam e-mails and harmful websites push a lot of malware, Trojans, and viruses toward computers on the network, independent of whether the enterprise is using a wireless or a wired network. If the attack is successful, the malware generally installs malicious code that runs in the background, capturing login information and keystrokes to relay it to the attackers.

Anytime someone visits a site requiring a login and a password such as Facebook, bank, payroll, or whatever, the malware harvests the information and sends it to the attacker. With this information, the attacker masquerades as the original user and does his evil activities.

Installing anti-malware and anti-virus protection on both non-mobile as well as mobile devices can ensure that such attacks do not take effect. To be more secure, these protection software programs must be run after every software install. In addition, keeping all programs and hardware up to date is a necessary step against e-mail phishing and spoofing.

EMPLOYEE EDUCATION IS NECESSARY

It pays to educate all employees of the organization to look out for attacks and to recognize one when they see it. It must start with a company-wide internet policy, letting employees know what acceptable and prohibited on-line activities are allowed in the company.

REFERENCES:

1. Sarna, S., Small Business Digest, *Simple Steps Businesses Can Take to Protect Themselves from Cyber Crime.* Available from: <http://www.2sbdigest.com/Protect-Themselves-from-Cyber-Crime>. [2013].

2. Lemos, R., Dark Reading, *10 Web Threats That Could Harm Your Business.* Available from: <http://www.darkreading.com/vulnerability/10-web-threats-that-could-harm-your-busi/240150315>. [15 March 2013].

3. Pullen, J.P., Enterprenuer, *How to Protect Your Small Business Against a Cyber Attack.* Available from: <http://www.entrepreneur.com/article/225468>. [27 February 2013].

PROTECTING AGAINST MOBILE DEVICE AND WIRELESS NETWORK ATTACKS

The RSA Conference at San Francisco recently discussed the most significant types of attacks that enterprises are now facing. It emerged that enterprises are facing increasing threats to mobile devices as attackers are taking advantage of the insecure consumer handsets, making them a pivot point for increasing their intrusions into the networks of enterprises.

As an example to one of the threats, one of the discussions was about how attackers pull down apps from one Android Marketplace, introduce a backdoor into it and sell it at another Android app store for a lower price. Even the Apple App Store is not foolproof against these malicious mobile applications, although it is difficult to bypass Apple's vetting process.

HOW IS AN ATTACK ON A MOBILE DEVICE A THREAT TO THE ENTERPRISE?

Attacks on mobile devices themselves, are not a direct threat to the enterprises. However, it becomes so when the attackers use the mobile devices to target the wired networks of enterprises. At this point, the mobile device becomes a real pivot vector. With different makes of mobile devices being available such as Apple, RIM, Android and Microsoft, the security models these organizations use for their products may have to be changed.

Attackers are now using sophisticated methods to infiltrate the network of enterprises. For instance, they package an iPhone with a high capacity battery and send it to their target organization via mail. Even if the package remains unopened, and the organization allows ad-hoc wireless connectivity to mobile devices, the iPhone will simply connect to the network and compromise it. The attacker then has a wide-open access to the network of their target enterprise.

Most attacks on mobile gadgets and wireless networks are successful since enterprises are not very restrictive in providing access to mobile devices. A reason for this is the demand from executives to allow unencumbered BYOD or bring-your-own-devices and allow them access to network resources.

WHAT ARE THE OTHER THREATS TO ENTERPRISES THROUGH THEIR WIRELESS NETWORKS?

Attackers take pride in their accomplishments and show it to the world. They attack the enterprise through hactivism, IPv6 and DNS. Most attackers use basic, easy-to-use tools to explore and exploit the weaknesses of their adversaries' defenses.

HOW TO THWART ATTACKS ON MOBILES AND WIRELESS NETWORKS

For wireless network security, the use of WLAN switches plays a major role. The switches can manage access to hundreds of points and are indispensable when setting up a secure enterprise wireless network.

For securing mobile devices in a better way, the enterprise must adopt a policy for deployment of secure mobile devices. A template for mobile device configuration helps in this regard. Additionally, the enterprise must also create a process for evaluating the mobile apps that could be used within the enterprise. The IT department can make sure the interaction of the device with the app makes functional sense. Administrators can keep their networks safe from the security threats coming from mobile devices, prevent spread of malware, and stop data theft, while the employees continue to use their devices.

In addition, the enterprise must employ a robust and secure wireless infrastructure. For more security, a segmented wireless network may be dedicated exclusively for mobile devices not cleared by the enterprise. The cost of a potential breach may be discussed as a strong point with decision makers within the enterprise to get them to agree on a separate wireless network.

Attackers are now using sophisticated malware to maintain connection with the DNS servers as long as the machine is able to resolve Internet domain names. Therefore, it is important to look for unusual DNS traffic and frequent barrages of requests on the Internet to unusual destinations.

Use of intrusion detection systems, malware detection systems and firewalls must be included in the network configuration and kept up-to-date for a defense-in-depth approach.

REFERENCES:

1. Eric B. Parizo, E. B., SearchSecurity, Mobile device attacks to enable more enterprise network intrusions. Available from: <http://searchsecurity.techtarget.com/news/2240118712/Mobile-device-attacks-to-enable-more-enterprise-network-intrusions>. [29 February 2012].

2. Phifer, L., Search Customization, Handheld and mobile device security: Mobile malware, breach prevention. Available from: <http://searchconsumerization.techtarget.com/tutorial/Handheld-and-mobile-device-security-Mobile-malware-breach-prevention>. [Feb 2010].

3. Gonsalves, A. Data Protection, Mobile devices set to become next DDoS attack tool. Available from: <http://www.csoonline.com/article/725382/mobile-devices-set-to-become-next-ddos-attack-tool>. [4 January 2013

INS AND OUTS OF CAPTCHA RE-RIDING ATTACKS

WHAT IS A CAPTCHA RE-RIDING ATTACK?

Many web sites want to distinguish whether it is a robot that is reading the site or a human, mostly to avoid the spread of spam. They use a system called CAPTCHA, which is an acronym for Completely Automated Public Turing Test to tell Computers and Humans Apart. The website has distorted text on the page, which can only be read by humans.

There are two types of CAPTCHA, one with a single word and one with two words. They mostly use old type fonts with deliberately introduced distortions to make it almost impossible for any OCR (Optical Character Recognition) to recognize. Therefore any automated system will not be able to bypass the CAPTCHA test. Websites use CAPTCHA when they want to avoid bogus memberships or hoax accounts. Some of the money related websites use it when creating new accounts. Some websites may test you with a CAPTCHA if you have entered a wrong password two or three times.

Attackers use the CAPTCHA re-riding attack to bypass the CAPTCHA protection, which the web applications adapt. In an HTTP session, the code for verifying the CAPTCHA solution sent by the user does not clear it; the attackers may exploit the situation. They use the same CAPTCHA solution to repeatedly send requests to the website.

WHAT HAPPENS DURING A CAPTCHA RE-RIDING ATTACK?

When a user visits a webpage and requests a registration the website creates an HTTP session, assigns it a session ID, and presents the registration page to the user along with the session ID inside a cookie. The registration page also has a tag, which directs the visitor's browser to a remote server to retrieve a CAPTCHA to be displayed on the screen.

The visitor's browser follows the instructions in the tag and sends a request to the remote server for the CAPTCHA. Accordingly, the server creates a new CAPTCHA with a random text and its solution, stores it for the current HTTP session and sends out the CAPTCHA image to the requesting client browser, to be displayed there.

The user solves the CAPTCHA and the browser sends the solution to the server for verification. The server retrieves its own solution from the HTTP session and verifies the solution with that provided by the client.

If the two solutions match, the client is given the clearance to proceed to the next logical step in the registration process; if the visitor's response doesn't match the CAPTCHA image, the registration process starts afresh.

During the verification process, the CAPTCHA solution remains inside the HTTP session and it is not cleared for as long as the session is alive. This is true if the verification succeeds and the user is cleared to the next step. If the verification fails, the web applications continue to use the same session ID and the same HTTP session. The attacker exploits this situation.

The attacker can solve the CAPTCHA and send the solution to the website, recording the submission using a web proxy. Using a custom script, or a tool such as Burp Intruder, he can send this request multiple times. With each request, he changes the User ID and is able to create multiple new accounts using the same single CAPTCHA solution, thus defeating the very purpose of having the CAPTCHA in the first place.

Instead of directly using them, attackers are exploiting the vulnerabilities to provide tools and data to others for illegal activities. Using such attacks, millions of harvested emails are often put up for sale, and these contain data related to military, government and intelligence agencies.

HOW TO PREVENT A CAPTCHA RE-RIDING ATTACK

Two major steps can prevent CAPTCHA re-riding attacks:

- Never trust emails from unknown recipients offering something you did not request and demanding your information;

- Reset the CAPTCHA solution within the HTTP session as soon as the CAPTCHA verification stage completes.

REFERENCES:

1. Kalra, G. S., Open Security Research, CAPTCHA Re-Riding Attack. Available from: <http://blog.opensecurityresearch.com/2012/02/captcha-re-riding-attack.html>. [28 February 2012].

2. Paganini, P., Security Affairs, The offer of Russian underground for phishing campaigns. Available from: <http://securityaffairs.co/wordpress/12756/

cyber-crime/the-offer-of-russian-underground-for-phishing-campaigns.html>. [9 March 2013].

3. Kalra, G. S., Blackhat.com, Bypassing CAPTCHAs by Impersonating CAPTCHA Providers. Available from: <https://media.blackhat.com/bh-us-12/Arsenal/Kalra/BH_US_12_Kalra_Bypassing_CAPTCHAs_by_Impersonating_CAPTCHA_Providers_WP.pdf>. [28 February 2012].

YOU NEED PATCH MANAGEMENT

WHAT IS PATCH MANAGEMENT?

One major time-consumer in business is to keep the infrastructure functional. For most businesses, the IT department spends more than 70% of its time in maintenance and administration, according to recent research from the International Data Corporation (IDC). For some, this figure is even higher, reaching 80% or more.

Updating, maintaining and patching software and systems for the latest security vulnerabilities are now major overhead expenses for IT managers. This is because IT systems are now more complex and distributed, and there is a significant increase in the overhead costs involved in keeping the systems functioning smoothly.

Software manufacturers release patch updates frequently, depending on how fast they are able to overcome vulnerabilities found in their programs. Not only software, but now firmware, development systems and hardware manufacturers also produce updates, and there are patches from software vendors and out-of-band patches to be handled.

WHY SHOULD PATCH MANAGEMENT BE A PRIORITY?

Most business' networks could carry a flaw in their unpatched systems, representing a real security threat. According to the US technology standards body, the NIST, in more than 90% of successful attacks against companies, the attackers exploited vulnerabilities that were already known. All the attacks could have been prevented had the systems been patched correctly and in time.

HOW SHOULD PATCH MANAGEMENT BE HANDLED?

IT departments in a business may decide to let users handle their own patch updates to reduce the company's IT burden. The real situation is not all patches released by their manufacturers install without creating further problems. There is risk of a breakup of critical business processes when users patch their systems with an untested patch. While off-the-shelf software is capable of being thus disrupted, it is more common with highly customized in-house software.

Centralized methods for patch management are therefore quickly catching up with businesses. For large businesses, the sheer numbers of servers, desktop systems, smartphones, tablets and all associated applications make it almost impossible to patch all devices manually. Automated systems of patch management handle such situations with more reliability and increased security.

Automated patch management can take care of the growing number of threats built specifically to attack systems before they are upgraded or patched. Many businesses and their IT security focus on mitigating the zero-day exploits, but human error in manual patching leaves too many systems vulnerable, even long after the patches have been released.

Manual and uncoordinated patching can leave the enterprise in a state of disruption and cause loss through downtime. This is mostly true in the case of patches untested for their compatibility with the operating software.

WHY AUTOMATED PATCHING IS AN ADVANTAGE TO BUSINESSES

Enterprises must implement in-house testing or look at using a patch supplier who also handles testing before applying patches on running systems. Although it does increase patch management cost deployment, the benefits far outweigh the investments due to the reduction in downtime and the consequent lost revenue.

Using automated patch management, the enterprise remains productive and conserves valuable IT resources. Most automated patch management systems can be programmed to implement patching beyond the core working time.

REFERENCES:

1. Lutz, S. Help Net Security, Automate your way out of patching hell. Available from: <http://www.net-security.org/article.php?id=1845>.[30 May 2013].

2. Florian, C., TechTalkToMe, 5 Benefits of Automating Patch Management. Available from: <http://www.gfi.com/blog/5-benefits-automating-patch-management/>. [25 November 2010].

3. Symantec, Automatic Patch Management. Available from: <http://www.symantec.com/articles/article.jsp?aid=automating_patch_management>. [8 February, 2005].

ARE YOUR WIRELESS DEVICES UNDER CONTROL?

WHAT IS THE THREAT?

Attackers gain illegal wireless access to an organization from outside the physical building. They bypass the security perimeters of the organization using wireless connections to internal access points. Attackers have initiated major thefts of data in this manner.

Wireless devices belonging to traveling officials are often infected by remote exploitation when used in a cyber cafe or during air travel. When reconnected to the network of the parent organization, the exploited devices are then used as back doors to gain access.

HOW DOES IT AFFECT BUSINESS?

Corporate security faces a huge threat from mobile devices, as concluded by a global study on mobility risks. The Ponemon Institute conducted the study sponsored by Websense in 2012. According to the study covering over 12 countries and 4,600 IT security practitioners, use of unsecured mobile devices led to data losses experienced by 51% of the organizations. More than 30% of the respondents experienced 50% more malware infection from these devices.

There were serious consequences of the data breach. Loss, removal and/or theft of information amounted to 38%, and an additional 38% went for disclosure of confidential or private data.

An attacker may use an unsecured wireless network for clandestine purposes such as spreading pornography. The breached organization, although not privy to such activity, may be drawn into legal wrangles.

Through unsecured wireless networks and devices, attackers can target Internet- banking services that usually send SMS authentication code for each online transaction. That makes it easy for the attacker to raid an account after stealing your login password.

HOW SHOULD RISKS BE MITIGATED?

It is impractical to expect employees not to use their wireless devices in public places such as a cyber cafe. The onus, therefore, is on the organization to mitigate the risks by extending all IT security and acceptable use policies to all mobile devices in the organization.

Rooted devices are easy to use as the user has full privileges to access all apps. However, this is true for the attacker as well, and rooted wireless devices should be refused access to the network.

To protect against data loss, full device encryption may be used along with provision for remote wipe, should a mobile device be stolen or lost. Encryption must be extended to any SD cards in use containing sensitive data.

Automated processes must be established for updating wireless devices so that they reflect the latest security fixes. Manufacturers of wireless devices provide security patches and the devices should be kept up to date.

Employees must be instructed to connect to Wi-Fi networks manually, instead of as peer-to-peer or ad hoc. This usually helps to prevent them from connecting to rogue networks specially designed for stealing information.

Instruct employees to disable file sharing before starting to use Wi-Fi hotspots or other unsecured wireless connections.

Wireless device users must make it a habit to disable the wireless connection on their device when not using them.

REFERENCES:

1. The SANS Institute, Critical Control 7: Wireless Device Control. Available from<http://www.sans.org/critical-security-controls/>. [June 2012].

2. Legnitto J., The Truth about Wi-Fi. Available from<http://www.privatewifi.com/are-your-employees-compromising-your-company%E2%80%99s-sensitive-information-with-unsecured-mobile-devices/>. [30 March 2012].

3. Prism Risk Assessment LLC. 2012. Available from<https://prismrm.wordpress.com/2012/12/27/unsecured-wireless-networks-can-bring-criminal-investigations-depending-on-who-is-using-it/>. [27 December 2012].

4. Sophos Ltd. Available from<http://www.sophos.com/en-us/medialibrary/PDFs/other/sophossecuritythreatreport2013.pdf> [2013].

HOW IS THE OZONE FRAMEWORK EXPECTED TO REVOLUTIONIZE THE HEALTHCARE INDUSTRY?

A mandate by the National Defense Authorization Act 2012 has declared the NSA project Ozone Widget Framework as open source.

THE OZONE WIDGET FRAMEWORK

The US Congress, along with the Department of Defense has recognized that OWF or the Ozone Widget Framework software helps effectively in the development and support of mission-critical applications. Originally, OWF was created as a platform for military command centers and used for web-based analytics. Today, health and disease management systems are using OWF increasingly.

OWF is a web application and it is open-source. As it is highly customizable, it assembles the tools required for accomplishing any task automatically, allowing the tools to communicate among themselves. The application is a framework permitting developers to select from a library of widgets that can perform specific functions for exchanging information; no special programming skills are required.

Widgets are a familiar feature thanks to their prolific use in tablets and smartphones. The most common example is Google MAPS and Voice Search is another. As developers are able to use OWF, through customization, they extend the layers for specific use. Anyone can extend or modify the code, since the software is open-source.

Using a dashboard, developers can easily select required widgets to build an application, which then acts as a web-portal for displaying the selected widgets in separate frames. Data exchange between different widgets happens in real time. According to NSA, OWF is under testing by the Army and the Navy internally, for creating a marketplace. Here, users can easily find and download applications. Using an Ozone software development kit, outside developers can write and publish their apps to the marketplace.

The key benefit form OWF comes in the form of rapid prototyping and integration of operational data and real-time intelligence. Since a widget is a visual component positioned on a board, the Table Widget provides visual representations of tabular data in a familiar tabular format. There can be one or more widgets individually displaying a section of the data for visualization.

For example, AppBoard has one or more widgets and presents the data objects visually, while running in the Flash Virtual Machine. There is no restriction on the display and it can contain any type of widget. That allows the system designer to present the data objects in the most suitable format that is of the utmost value to the end-user. Widgets may typically be of the type:

- Graph or Chart
- Table or Data Grid

- Topological Map for representing the structure of a network

- Geographical Map for displaying data overlaid on a map

THE OZONE WIDGET FRAMEWORK IN HEALTH INFORMATION SYSTEMS

Typically, problems with Big Data means the inability to analyze large volumes in real time as rapidly increasing information is collected across disparate systems. That additionally means no communication of the analysis exists across different types of users.

In the past, systems collected data and processed them in information silos, while analysts used separate applications and output formats. The method was time consuming and at best, it was a past-view model of the situation. Since the Internet is now a dominant means for data sharing, applications use XML and similar standards for interpreting and communicating different data types. File based data, after morphing from database platforms to relational databases, is currently moving towards columnar-based systems.

Big Data problems are further compounded by the explosion of devices connecting through IP addresses rather than via people. For example, the Internet of Things is transforming data analytics in several innovative ways:

- Genomists in the area of disease and health information are using different systems for accumulating and exchanging scientific data. By adopting the OWF platform, they can use a single metadata repository for connecting and analyzing information through a single portal.

- European CDC is testing epidemic intelligence using OWF for monitoring health data collected from various networks and several medical facilities.

- Emerging countries are expanding telemedicine health-care along with smartphone apps taking advantage of cellular communication, since that provides a cost effective way to capture, analyze and share patient data.

- OWF, slated to operate on smartphones and tablets in the future, can help doctors in serology, diagnosis of diseases and data collection via CAT, PET and X-ray images.

- OWF applications are finding growth markets in implant devices with remote monitoring features. Diabetes control, pulmonary edema monitoring, heart pacemakers and implants for detecting the onset of seizures can create substantial data flows that a standard set of widgets can display for analysis. Since OWF is capable of supporting data captured from sensors in the field, it can support similar requirement in health monitoring.

CONCLUSION:

OWF is not unique, since the market place has several web portal information systems. However, it is valuable as it is open source, reflecting significant investments from the US taxpayers and it can now be applied to solving healthcare information stranded with Big Data problems. The challenge will come from the for-profit health-care providers - whether they will be willing to adhere to a common platform for information exchange and data analysts across the chain of healthcare providers, insurers and public agencies.

ATTACKS VIA USB

WHAT IS AN ATTACK VIA USB?

Although USB devices help computer operators simplify their storage and transfer problems in a myriad of ways, they are also the most common devices for delivery of malware.

The main process of malware delivery via USB happens because of the AutoRun feature in Windows, which allows any executable file on the USB device to be automatically detected and launched.

Any infected USB device, it could be a mobile phone, a flash drive, an mp3 player, digital camera or a PSP, can start an executable file, which then lets in a wide array of malware into the computer. The damaging malware then makes its way into the core of the Windows operating system, and begins replicating itself every time the computer restarts.

Although AutoRun is a very useful feature in Windows, it helps spread more than two-thirds of current malware. Thankfully, Auto-Play has replaced it. This feature asks the user if he/she would like to run the executable file it has detected on the USB device, and offers other choices such as opening the folder to view the files. A similar feature is available in Macintosh computers, and this is more secure than the Window's AutoRun. Linux straightaway displays the folders and has no AutoRun feature, making it somewhat safer than the other two. However, the threat from the USB devices goes deeper than AutoRun.

HOW DOES THE ATTACKER GAIN ACCESS VIA USB?

Attackers use the USB port in different ways for implementing their nefarious activities. One of the simpler ways is to let in an executable file through the AutoRun feature of Windows, or to entice the user to execute it when AutoPlay offers various choices. However, scanning the USB medium with an anti-virus or an anti-malware program can eliminate most malware if the AutoRun feature is turned off.

The other way attackers gain access is less obvious and there is really no easy method of stopping or preventing the attack. An attacker could be an insider, such as a disgruntled employee, intent on stealing information to pass on to a business competitor. The attacker attaches a USB dongle to the computer. This dongle sits between the keyboard and the computer, and all keystrokes the user makes, pass through the dongle. Since the dongle does not add any software to the computer, it remains undetected by the anti-virus and anti-malware programs. Being physically small and residing behind the computer, the dongle goes virtually undetected.

The dongle collects keystrokes the user makes and stores them in its memory. When the dongle is removed and the attacker analyzes it, he gains access to all the passwords and usernames of the owner of the computer. The attacker can then use this information any way he likes.

In some cases, the USB dongle masquerades as a keyboard and a mouse, and there is no way any anti-virus or anti-malware can block it. The user's keystrokes are surreptitiously passed to the attacker through the USB dongle via browser and internet connection. The attacker then has full control of the user's computer.

HOW TO PREVENT ATTACKS FROM THE USB

Unless you are sure of the USB device, **never start your computer with the USB device attached**. This accounts for 60% of malware to gain access to the computer before any anti-virus or anti-malware program can even start up.

Have a company-wide policy of allowing only permitted USB devices to operate on the computer. Other non-permitted USB devices will be detected and blocked. This is possible by altering the Registry in Windows and adding suitable scripts to Mac and Linux computers.

Have better security for physical access to sensitive computers and to their USB ports. Restricting access to the USB port eliminates this threat.

REFERENCES:

1. Savvas, M., Computerworld UK, *Cybercrooks Use USB Devices in Attacks.* Available from: <http://www.techhive.com/article/209853/cybercrooks_use_usb_devices_in_attacks.html>. [7 November 2010].

2. Caroll, S., PC Mag.com, *USB Malware Attacks On the Rise.* Available from: <http://www.pcmag.com/article2/0,2817,2372152,00.asp>. [4 November 2010].

3. Mills, E., CNET, *Researchers turn USB cable into attack tool.* Available from: <http://news.cnet.com/8301-27080_3-20028919-245.html>. [19 January 2011].

4. Beccaonline.org, *The Evolution of USB Based Microcontroller Attacks in Corporate Espionage.* Available from: <http://www.becca-online.org/images/The_Evolution_of_USB_Based_Microcontroller_Attacks_in_Corporate_Espionage.pdf>. [?].

5. Crenshaw, A., Irongeek.com, *Plug and Prey: Malicious USB Devices*. Available from: <http://www.irongeek.com/i.php?page=security/plug-and-prey-malicious-usb-devices>. [2011].

CHALLENGES IN MOBILE HEALTH

CHALLENGES IN MOBILE HEALTH

Advances in mobile health can be estimated from the $750+ million invested in venture capital in companies. Several corporate giants such as Microsoft, Qualcomm, Apple and Samsung are turning out smartphones capable of capturing medical-quality images of the inner ear or measuring blood pressure, creating mobile health products and investing in startups.

The basic idea is to capture all kinds of data for improving health care. The increasing number of smartphones and associated small, inexpensive sensors along with low-energy Bluetooth and analytical software enable patients to play a more active role in their own health. Simultaneously, nurses and doctors can make house calls without leaving their offices.

However, mobile health technology can be tricky to implement. Wristbands for activity tracking, made by one of the most well known firms, had to be recalled after users complained of skin irritation from wearing it. Measuring blood glucose levels without drawing blood, is still not available because of technological difficulties, although this is a desirable feature for people with diabetes.

On the other hand, there have been technological achievements as well. Mobile phones have helped increase activity among patients with diabetes. Activity monitors provided feedback that combined with existing records of patients, while an algorithm determined the text message to be sent to the patients. Those falling behind in achieving their goals received messages of encouragement. Based on location data from the mobile device some patients received information about nearby aerobics classes or about different ways to exercise indoors. After six months, not only was the average patient walking about a mile farther each day, their blood sugar control had improved significantly.

The success of the above program has two sides. Patients are healthier, translating into a lower cost of caring for them for partners. Usually, payoffs for better managing diabetes, a chronic disease, comes over many years. However, in this case, many patients were able to drop their blood sugar and that equates to savings of $1000 to $1200 in doctor visits and other treatments. Since the program costs $300 per patient to run, the return on the program is substantial.

Based on such results, enthusiasts are convinced that mobile technology can successfully overhaul the delivery of health care. They also estimate that mobile technology will offer sufficient financial benefits so that patients and insurers will be convinced to pay for it.

However, patients are not so easily convinced. Although 10 percent of Americans own a type of tracking device to measure the quality of their sleep, calorie intake or monitor the steps they take, more than half of them no longer use devices. Even when there are more than 100,000 mobile health applications available for smartphones, only a few have been downloaded more than 500 times. Additionally, of those who have downloaded such an application, more than two-thirds have stopped using it.

One reason for the slow enthusiasm has been unrealistic expectation from current imperfect technology. For example, simple functions such as step counting lack precision. Another reason is many people lacked motivation and simply did not take to using these devices and applications. Evidently, a well-designed mobile health system does help provided patients use it.

THE MHEALTH MARKETPLACE AND SMARTPHONES

As of 2014, there were upwards of 140 million smartphones in the US and this number is expected to cross the 200 million mark in the next five years. Thousands of applications are fueling this growth, empowering users in their daily lives. Now consumers can conveniently deposit checks, avoid traffic snarls, play games and stay in touch with their friends, all from their handheld convenience.

However, the US healthcare infrastructure has been rather slow in embracing the non-traditional physician-patient encounter. Very few among the US population have ever used telemedicine, one of mHealth technologies. Although solutions are prevalent in other service-based industries such as travel, insurance and banking, the healthcare industry faces several hurdles when implementing mHealth. For example, extremely few numbers of smartphone users have ever received an email or alert directly related to their health.

An insight into the state of mHealth can be gained from existing mHealth apps. These can be divided into three types of encounters:

1. The patient initiates and concludes the encounter

2. The healthcare provider initiates and concludes the encounters

3. Either initiates the encounter, but the other concludes it.

In the first two encounters, either the patient or the physician can utilize technology personally to meet their medical needs. For example, a physician may look up the dose for a medication or the patient may track his or her blood pressure. In both examples, the physician and the patient are not dependent upon each other.

The third encounter is a much tougher model, as some pre-coordination must exist before action can be taken on data being collected. Here, the patient or physician initiates the app use and the other concludes the interaction.

Given the enormous number of medical apps and mobile platforms prevailing, it is hardly surprising that there exists a lack of standardization. For example, a patient may opt to use a diabetes app without consulting or coordinating with their physician. In the next in-person visit, the physician may only be able to adjust the diabetes regimen by reviewing the paper printout that the patient brought. That marginalizes the value of collecting that data in real time. Had the patient and the physician been able to share data in real time, review it and act on it, complications could be prevented before they had time to arise.

The process of adopting mHealth can also run into logistical hurdles with financial ramifications. For example, a primary care professional managing a population of 2,000 patients may not have adequate resources to integrate and act upon daily notifications that could easily run into hundreds. Modern utility grids are designed to adjust their workflow by foreseeing and managing the peaks and troughs of power consumption. However, healthcare practices, especially the brick-and-mortar type, are fragmented and were not initially designed to work in that manner. Moreover, a utility company has financial incentives for delivering energy efficiently – they save money and improve their margins. For healthcare, unfortunately, there are no financial incentives for either the patient or the physician who want to invest their resources into several discrete mHealth solutions.

Most independent physician practices are unable to invest in new infrastructure because they lack resources. A local barbershop would consider it worthless to invest in a special app that costs thousands of dollars only for allowing customers to book online appointments and get reminders when it is already running to maximum capacity. In healthcare also, a family physician practice operating at capacity, will be reluctant to welcome additional patients and risk decreasing its already wafer-thin margins by investing in new services.

PUBLIC HEALTH, LARGE SCALE HEALTH CARE AND MHEALTH

The level of computing capacity available in even basic cell phones and their high penetration makes this a potential technology for creating significant differences to public health and health care delivery. Researchers can use the mHealth technologies to capture multiple sources of health data. This could include, for example, in-depth information about the environment for GWAS or genome-wide association studies; location and travel areas; detailed information about the physical activities of subjects; physiological responses through sensors attached to the body; and activities through text messaging surveys over extended periods of time.

Further, mHealth methodologies with highly accessible data availability can be utilized to alter public health and health care on a large scale. For example, remote areas without easy physical access routes for physicians can be monitored and health care dispensed with through mHealth technologies. Employing mobile tools can decrease the number of people who develop diabetes through ignorance, prevent accidents at home and help remind people to take their medication as scheduled.

More consumers are now aware of and demand health apps and sensors. However, consumers are still in the process of coming to terns regarding the benefits, risks and impact of these apps and sensors on health outcomes – positive, neutral or negative. The main issues hampering the efforts are privacy, confidentiality, regulatory control, protection to the human subject, logistics and interoperability among carriers. For creating safe, scalable and effective health programs, researchers will need to develop and assess the entire spectrum of mHealth technologies.

CONCLUSION

Mobile healthcare offers an important extension to electronic health care. With mHealth, caregivers are able to gain uninterrupted access to the clinical data of their patients and the latest in medical knowledge. Concurrently, patients with chronic conditions can remain under constant observation without leaving their homes. Full-scale implementation of mHealth involves solving critical challenges such as developing better display technologies, establishing interoperability among electronic health records and security controls for mobile devices. It also requires developing smart algorithms for detecting clinically significant events and subsequently informing caregivers.

Mobile health is opening up new opportunities for personalized healthcare and joint decision-making with physician-patient relationships. However, several new challenges are also coming up – ensuring confidentiality of patient data, empowering patients with medical knowledge in everyday language and most importantly, mindset adjustment of both patients and caregivers.

REFERENCES

1. mHealth - Mobile Health Technologies http://obssr. od.nih.gov/scientific_areas/methodology/mhealth/

2. Mobile Technology and Health Care, From NIH Director Dr. Francis S. Collins http://www.nlm.nih.gov/medlineplus/magazine/issues/winter11/articles/winter11pg2-3. html

3. Why Mobile Health Technologies Haven't Taken Off (Yet) http://www.forbes.com/sites/robertszczerba/2014/07/16/ why-mobile-health-technologies-havent-taken-off-yet/

4. Mobile Health's Growing Pains http://www. technologyreview.com/news/529031/ mobile-healths-growing-pains/

TARGETED BOTNET ATTACKS AND YOUR RESPONSE

Since 15 April 2013, more than 90,000 computers have together attacked the WordPress website hosted by CloudFlare and Hostgator. All users of WordPress, with username "admin" were targeted and more than 10 million random passwords were tried every minute to gain access to their accounts. This targeted attack of the botnets is one of the most powerful ever to be waged on WordPress.

WHAT ARE BOTNETS?

Cyber criminals infiltrate a computer by placing a malware inside it. That turns the computer into a bot, also called a drone or a zombie. The malware resides within the operating system, camouflaging itself from the anti-virus and anti-malware security programs and multiplying itself whenever files from the infected computer are transferred to another computer, infecting the second computer as well. Very soon, it infects several computers in a row and connects all of them via the Internet to form a botnet, which then comes under the control of the botmaster.

HOW BOTNETS AFFECT COMPUTERS

Botnets use a coordinated brute force attack, flooding the targeted server with countless login requests. The botnets try various combinations of usernames and passwords to gain entry, and own the user's accounts they can break into. The attack usually slows down the servers and users on the server are locked out of their websites. This is called the DDoS or the Direct Denial of Service. As Word-Press users are given a username "Admin" while they use a password of their own choice, the botnet that attacked the WordPress servers went after users who had not changed their original username.

Once a computer is compromised, it forms another bot and becomes a part of the botnet. The botmaster can extract any information from the compromised machine. Impressive numbers of computers in a targeted attack have the ability to inflict real damage. A single IP or a few IPs can be easily blocked out, but it becomes a different matter when a substantially large number of IPs (above 90,000 in the attack on WordPress) are involved. Attack from multiple computers can be timed to occur several times a second (trying as many as over two billion passwords an hour), overwhelming the security at the server they have targeted.

WHY DO BOTNETS ATTACK COMPUTER SERVERS?

Botnets are constantly trying to increase their numbers so that they can create the condition of an overwhelming flood when they attack. In their quest for adding more computers to their botnets, botmasters target servers with more users attached. Botmasters went after Wordpress as, unlike most home computers, servers hosting WordPress blogs are some of the best in processing power.

Any botmaster setting up a botnet seeks powerful computers. A botnet of such computers can be far more powerful than a regular home-computer constituted botnet, and can then launch DDoS attacks of far greater intensity than what is normally witnessed.

More than 60 million websites around the world are hosted on WordPress, and botmasters would have tremendous computing power if they were able to control even a fraction of these sites.

HOW CAN YOU PREVENT YOUR OWN SITE FROM BEING COMPROMISED BY BOTNETS?

Although the botnets use brute force to try to gain control, it is relatively easy to hold them off. In the case of WordPress users, they had to change their username from "admin" to something different, and at the same time, make their passwords stronger by using a combination of numbers, letters and special characters.

Use of two-step authentication can be another deterrent against botnet attacks. Although it increases the annoyance while logging on to sites like WordPress, it makes it easier for the servers to detect that you are not a bot before they log you on. This makes your site far more secure.

CloudFlare, the server that hosts WordPress, offers free plans that guarantee automatic block for any login attempt that looks like it is from a botnet.

Use the latest released version of the application, as WordPress has already blocked security holes that attackers were exploiting.

REFERENCES:

1. BBC, News Technology, *WordPress website targeted by hackers*. Available from: <http://www.bbc.co.uk/news/technology-22152296>. [15 April 2013].

2. Wheately, M., siliconANGLE, *How To Sidestep The WordPress Botnet Hack*. Available from: <http://siliconangle.com/blog/2013/04/15/how-to-sidestep-the-wordpress-botnet-hack/>. [15 April 2013].

3. Vincent, J., The Independent, *$500 million botnet Citadel attacked by Microsoft and the FBI.* Available from: <http://www.independent.co.uk/life-style/gadgets-and-tech/news/500-million-botnet-citadel-attacked-by-microsoft-and-the-fbi-8647594.html>. [6 June 2013].

SECURE CONFIGURATIONS VIGILANCE

THE EXTENT OF THE THREAT

When attackers have compromised both the external and internal networks of an enterprise, they usually install automated computer attack programs that constantly scan the target networks. These programs search for systems that have vulnerable software installed in the default configuration, as delivered from resellers and manufacturers.

As default configurations are mostly meant for ease-of-deployment and ease-of-use rather than security, these are exploitable in their default state. Moreover, security patches are not always applied in a planned manner. Software updates too, often introduce unknown weaknesses into vulnerable software that attackers can exploit.

EFFECT ON THE ENTERPRISE

Once attackers have gained access to the network, they are able to trespass within, approach, store data in the system or retrieve data from it, communicate with, intercept, interfere or change the system at will.

It is easy for them to obstruct the network services by planting malicious programs and overloading the resources. This might fill up hard drive storage space, send messages for resetting a host's subnet mask, as well as preventing network resources from accepting network connections.

Attackers can also use the system as a pivot point for invading further into the enterprise. Common forms of attack include distributed denial of service, relay of worms, viruses, or spam and destruction or modification of files.

It is easy for the attackers to plant a program, which is undetectable (such a program is called a Trojan Horse), into an unauthorized application and use it to siphon money from the enterprise accounts or transfer credit card numbers or trade secrets to remote servers.

The risks faced by the enterprise include:

- Unauthorized disclosure of information
- Disruption of computer services
- Loss of productivity
- Financial loss
- Legal implications
- Blackmail

Not only does the enterprise lose confidential and sensitive information, it is also subject to loss of credibility, reputation, competitive edge and market share. Customers, investors or even the public may sue the enterprise for the security or privacy breaches.

HOW CAN THIS THREAT BE MITIGATED?

The best way to avoid security breaches is to prevent them from happening in the first place, by adopting and employing a strong security policy for the enterprise.

Although 100% of breaches or leaks cannot be prevented, it is possible to minimize the damages and remediate effectively. Using secure configuration for all your hardware and software assets along with inventory control and management can help to achieve this.

This also requires proper deployment, maintenance and documentation of layered security architecture for protecting the enterprise network. A layered architecture would include, apart from access controls, firewalls, antivirus tools and encrypted data transmissions, and the advanced analysis and detection capabilities of technology such as sandbox.

By employing sandbox technologies, the enterprise has the knowledge base to detect, identify and to defend against new threats as they arrive and

remediate as necessary. An additional advantage with sandboxing is documenting the steps taken by the enterprise for complying with the guidelines of the SEC breach disclosure.

REFERENCES:

1. Sans Institute, *Critical Control 3: Secure Configurations for Hardware and Software on Mobile Devices, Laptops, Workstations, and Servers.* Available from: <http://www.sans.org/critical-security-controls/control.php?id=3>. [2013].

2. Hau, D., Sans Institute, *Unauthorized Access – Threats, Risk, and Control.* Available from: <http://www.giac.org/paper/gsec/3161/unauthorized-access-threats-risk-control/105264>. [11 July 2013].

3. Threattracksecurity.com, *Enterprise security white paper sandboxing helps avoid security breach.* Available from: <http://www.threattracksecurity.com/documents/enterprise-security-white-paper-sandboxing-helps-avoid-security-breach.pdf>. [2013].

IDENTIFYING AND PROTECTING AGAINST MOBILE WEB HACKING

WHAT IS MOBILE WEB HACKING?

You may suddenly discover that personal information from your mobile is splattered all over the Internet. Possibly your text messages, your pictures and intimate conversations are available for all to see. Not only is this an invasion of privacy, it may also be extremely damaging to your livelihood and personal life.

In the technologically advanced world, sometimes people want to hack into personal details of others for various reasons. For example, there may be people who you have fallen out with in business or love, people who may dislike you for something you have said or done, or friends who have now become unfriendly. It is prudent to guard your personal information properly, as it is not always possible to predict how some relationships might turn out.

Apart from sour relationships, business rivalry is another reason for mobile web hacking. Your business competitor may want access to your personal information to know what you may be planning next. There may also be the friendly neighborhood attacker who wants to blackmail you over some sensitive information you have in your cellphone. The attacker may also be looking for your financial information to steal from your bank account.

HOW TO DETERMINE IF YOUR MOBILE HAS BEEN HACKED

Most users of mobile devices do not think of their cellphones as computers and hence do not take adequate steps to protect them as they do their PCs and laptops.

Mobile devices are increasingly becoming as powerful and sophisticated as regular computers, and hence are equally vulnerable unless protected adequately. When an attacker compromises a system, he has to tamper with the mobile's system files in some way to prevent detection and to maintain continued access. This may include deleting some files, replacing or altering them, or even adding extra files.

Intrusion detection systems or IDS can warn you if there are attempts by attackers to penetrate your cellphone. Periodic file integrity checking is one method of identifying if your mobile has been hacked and/or compromised by an attacker slipping past your IDS.

People are increasingly using smart mobile phones to visit websites and conduct several types of transactions on the web. It is very easy for attackers to compromise a mobile phone after the user has visited an infected or hacked website.

Detecting an infected site is easy with the Google Webmaster Tool or GWT, which has warnings for malware. When the tool detects malware, it sends warning emails to the webmaster and owners can see the warning when they login via the Webmaster Tool.

HOW CAN YOU PROTECT YOURSELF FROM MOBILE WEB HACKING?

- Download apps only from your phone's store;
- Update to the latest operating system of your phone and the installed apps;
- Always have your firewall turned on;
- Install the latest antivirus software and update it regularly;
- Install the latest antispyware program and update it regularly;
- Never download from suspicious websites;
- Never open suspicious looking attachments to emails;
- Turn on Bluetooth only when necessary;
- Turn off your phone when not in use for long.

It is imperative to treat your phone as a computer and protect it in the same manner. One of the most important tips is to keep your mobile with you always or in a place where you know it will be safe, and not leave it around in a public place. It is also prudent not to store too much sensitive information in your phone, and keep track of what kind of data or photos you maintain.

REFERENCES:

1. Cobb, M., ComputerWeekly.com, *How to detect hacking with a Microsoft file integrity checker*. Available from: <http://www.computerweekly.com/tip/How-to-detect-hacking-with-a-Microsoft-file-integrity-checker>. [Nov 2010].

2. Rana, G., Gogi.in, *How to Detect if your Website is Hacked or Infected.* Available from: <http://www.gogi.in/detect-website-hacked-infected.html>. [7 December 2011].

3. Mardigian-Kiles, T., Webroot, *How to Prevent Phone Hacking and Sleep Like a Baby Again.* Available from: <http://www.webroot.com/En_US/consumer/articles/mobile-how-to-prevent-phone-hacking-and-sleep-like-a-baby-again>. [2004].